Exploring Toronto

by The Toronto Chapter of Architects

GREEY
dePENCIER
BOOKS

First edition   1972
Second and Third printing 1973
Fourth and Fifth printing 1974
Sixth printing   1975
Revised edition   1977

©Greey de Pencier Publications
59 Front Street East
Toronto, Ontario

Printed in Canada 1977

Editor: Annabel Slaight
Art Director: Ron Butler
Cover Photo: Garth Scheuer
Maps: Barry Craig

ISBN 0-919872-28-X

Notes about the maps
*If you are exploring Toronto for the first time, we feel it would be useful for you
to purchase one of the many available comprehensive street maps as a companion
to this book. The architect-authors produced our maps as a guide to things to see
and do rather than to detail specific information about city travel. Our maps help
you discover Toronto but don't always tell you what streetcar to catch.*

*Now about street names. In preparing this book we found out all sorts of con-
troversies about spelling. For example, three different "official" sources claimed
three different "official" spellings for one of the escarpment streets — Tyrel,
Tyrrel and Tyrrell. We chose Tyrel because that's how the street sign read. But,
we encountered this again and again, so consider this tiny element of surprise as
one of Toronto's many delights.*

80-4000

Contents

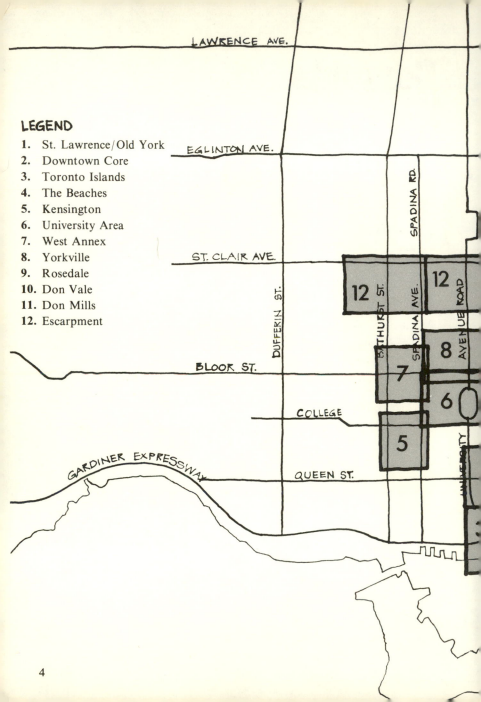

LEGEND

1. St. Lawrence/Old York
2. Downtown Core
3. Toronto Islands
4. The Beaches
5. Kensington
6. University Area
7. West Annex
8. Yorkville
9. Rosedale
10. Don Vale
11. Don Mills
12. Escarpment

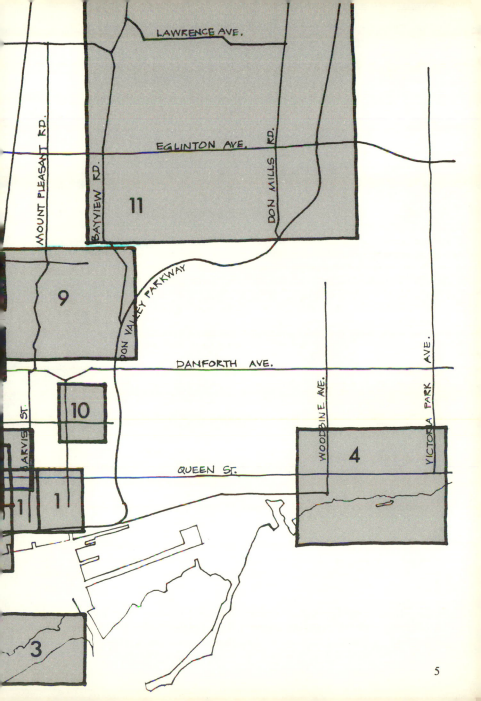

LAWRENCE AVE.

MOUNT PLEASANT RD.

BAYVIEW RD.

EGLINTON AVE.

DON MILLS RD.

11

DON VALLEY PARKWAY

9

DANFORTH AVE.

WOODBINE AVE.

VICTORIA PARK AVE.

ST.

10

JARVIS ST.

QUEEN ST.

4

1

1

3

5

About the architect~authors

Eric Arthur, professor emeritus of architecture at the University of Toronto, is well known for his contribution to our early architecture as well as his part in the restoration of St. Lawrence Hall and Enoch Turner Schoolhouse. A Companion of the Order of Canada and one of the founders of the Architectural Conservancy of Ontario, he is now acting as a consultant on the restoration of University College at the University of Toronto.

Ron Thom is a rare Canadian architect. He came to the profession with an art school background and no formal architectural training. Nevertheless, he has swept up numerous design awards in British Columbia and Ontario. His best known projects include Trent University in Peterborough and Massey College at the University of Toronto.

Erland Gustavs, who long rated Stockholm (where he studied on a Canada Council grant) and Paris as his favorite cities, now rejoices in the vitality of Toronto. Architect, planner, lecturer (at University of Waterloo), and interior designer, his work includes a medical centre in California, land planning in Delaware, offices in the Toronto core, and a corporate identity program for an airline.

Roger du Toit, originally from South Africa, is an architect and planner practicing in Toronto. He has worked on such major projects as Metro Centre, for Toronto's waterfront; and Erin Mills, a new town outside Toronto. He has participated in developing design guidelines for the City of Toronto's downtown core and has also found time for active participation in citizen and professional groups. He is a year-round resident of the Toronto Islands, and says he loves it.

Jack Klein, author of the Beaches chapter, has a national reputation as a design specialist in medium density multiple housing environments and in urban renewal. He has several books on these subjects to his credit and his firm, Klein and Sears, has won many top prizes for architectural design.

Jerome Markson and his enthusiasm about Toronto were guiding forces behind publication of this book. It was his perseverance while president of the Toronto Chapter of Architects that actually got the project underway. Markson was born and educated in Toronto and has been building his own successful architectural practice here since 1955.

Andrew Clarke, co-author of the Kensington chapter, had the distinction in 1970 of becoming the youngest registered architect in Ontario. He is a graduate of the University of Toronto and has been with Jerome Markson Architects since 1967. He has been actively involved in Toronto Chapter of Architects affairs.

George Baird writes about U. of T. from many years first-hand experience. As well as having studied there, he has been teaching in the School of Architecture since 1968. In addition to his professorial duties, Baird has a burgeoning architectural practice and has authored several books. He is now completing a philosophical history of architectural ideas.

James Acland, before his untimely death in 1976, was professor of architectural history at the University of Toronto and one of Toronto's most ardent defenders of significant old buildings. He was president of the Ontario Architectural Conservancy, chairman of the Friends of Old City Hall and his dedication to this work will be long remembered. Professor Acland's publications include *Medieval Structure, The Gothic Vault.*

Jack Diamond, since his arrival here in 1964 from South Africa, has become one of the city's most eloquent spokesmen for urban quality. He is involved in community groups, appears on TV, and has written numerous articles. His busy practice in architecture and urban planning involves projects which exemplify the principles of architecture and planning he espouses. His office is in a recycled warehouse of his design.

Eberhard Zeidler came to Canada from Germany in 1951. Since then, as partner in charge of design for Zeidler Partnership Architects, he has established an international reputation for such trend-setting architecture as the Eaton Centre and Ontario Place here in Toronto and the McMaster Health Sciences Centre in Hamilton. Zeidler lives in a ravine setting in Rosedale on Beaumont Road.

Irving Grossman has designed many types of award-winning buildings but his trail-blazing has largely been in the residential field. He was architect-planner for the initial phase of Flemingdon Park and more recently created the Edgeley Village community. He can be called a true Torontonian — he grew up right in the heart of the city.

John C. Parkin, senior partner of the Toronto-based Parkin Partnership Architects Planners, is one of Canada's best known architects. He has been honored for service both by his profession and his country. He is a Companion of the Order of Canada, and holds the degrees Master in Architecture and Doctor of Engineering. He has designed buildings in the four corners of the world but a good cross-section can be seen in the Don Mills area.

Colin Vaughan is a skilled advocate on many urban issues but is perhaps best known for his vigorous campaign against the Spadina Expressway. As an architect, he was a partner in the firm of Robbie, Vaughan and Williams, creators of the Canadian pavilion for Expo '67. In 1972 he was elected a City of Toronto alderman. He has lived on the escarpment since 1959.

Foreword: Notes on the City

For a long time I have thought Toronto to be a most exciting city to live in or to visit.

In that view, I was ahead of those who, since Anna Jameson in the 1830s, thought Toronto subject for jest — Toronto's Sunday was compared, often unfavorably, with Sunday in Puritan England in the 17th century, or with Belfast in the 20th century where children's playgrounds are chained and locked. An old friend once even published a book, which, if I remember rightly, was called *Let's All Hate Toronto*. When I came back from England in 1941, I wrote that I saw more evidence of bombing downtown than I had seen in any town in England except Coventry and London. I referred, of course, to parking lots. There are fewer today, as the central core is gradually being built up. Development will inevitably move east and west, especially if land is made available over the railway tracks. This will provide an opportunity for the city to designate land for parks, an amenity which we, among cities in the western world, rank low. The skyline is pierced with highrise hotels and owners of banks and insurance companies vie with each other in reaching for the heavens, offering rare marble in their lobbies and choice wood interiors from the remote forests of the world.

In 1963 I wrote in *Toronto — No Mean City:* "Only yesterday I saw that the City Hall had risen high above the surrounding board fence and, from the seventh floor of a Bay Street building, the staff could see the great central column and the tremendous sweep of the curved enclosing walls. It will be a supremely great building in terms of function and the monumentality of its public spaces, but one would like to forecast that it will also be an edifice where citizens for centuries can see all that was best in art in this generation. It is a challenge for the artists of Canada, but no greater than for the artists who worked on the Town Hall in Stockholm, in smaller, less rich and less populated Sweden. This writer is confident that they will meet it." A mural by David Partridge is a happy beginning.

Every city is entitled to one folly and, for a long time, we enjoyed Casa Loma. But now, we have a second — 1,815 feet, 5 inches high costing $50 million dollars — the CN Tower. The owners would not call it a folly because, if heights don't bother you, you can eat there, and facilities are

Casa Loma stables

Firehall Theatre

St. James Cathedral

provided for UHF and VHF television microwave transmission and fixed mobile systems. For all of that, $50M seems a good buy!

A most encouraging trend in recent years is the interest taken by young architects and young politicians in our old buildings. Except for such obvious monuments as Osgoode Hall, St. James' Cathedral and University College, we are getting to the bottom of the historical building barrel. Two fine old buildings of 1822 and 1848 — Chief Justice Campbell's house, moved to University Avenue, and Enoch Turner Schoolhouse on Trinity Street — have by a miracle, plus hard work, been preserved. Not threatened so far are my favorite churches — St. Paul's United, 121 Avenue Rd., (a superb art nouveau interior), old St. Paul's at 83 Power St., Maurice Cody Hall on Bloor E., and St. Anne's, Gladstone Ave. in which some of the Group of Seven painters left their mark as a labor of love. The old City Hall has been saved, but the future of Union Station, bathed in golden lamp

light at night, is still uncertain. Remarkable, too, is the continued existence of the Church of the Holy Trinity, a charming collection of historic buildings, now completely engulfed by the giant complex of the Eaton Centre. Not yet landscaped, it will prove an oasis for the footsore and weary shopper, with equal benefit to the store and the church. The visitor should look to the balcony on Scadding House because it was from there that Dr. Scadding, Toronto's great historian, once gazed on the city he loved as far south as the Islands, and east to the bluffs at Scarborough.

To get the true flavor of this cosmopolitan city, all visitors should see our two markets: St. Lawrence, which goes back to 1803 (though not the building it's housed in) and the Kensington. The former is a farmers' market, orderly and beautiful, and English is spoken almost to the exclusion of other languages. It is the total opposite of the nervous, colorful, disorderly Kensington, where in a babel of tongues, English can be heard

Unique view of Toronto-Dominion Centre

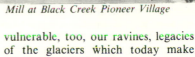

Mill at Black Creek Pioneer Village

only as a still small voice. Both markets are great fun, and a regular meeting place for friends.

This is not the place to compare our architecture with that of Montreal, except to praise Montreal for its subway stations. The trains are quiet and the stations were designed by young architects who showed an obvious pride in their transit system and their city. Toronto stations were well described by a *Globe and Mail* editorial writer who said they belonged to the public lavatory school of thought. In 1976, stations were brightened by fine tile in a variety of colored patterns. We now have the cleanest subway stations in the world, and the best-maintained trains where, in the uncrowded hours, knitting is a popular pursuit and 50 percent of the passengers read. You won't find that elsewhere in North America.

How fortunate we are with The Islands, but how vulnerable they are to the whims of insensitive, irresponsible politicians who cannot bear to leave them in their natural state. How vulnerable, too, our ravines, legacies of the glaciers which today make admirable sites for apartment houses, or the garage of an insurance company — a recent obstruction on a site inviolate for 10 million years.

On the positive side, how singularly fortunate are we in our Museum, which has one of the great collections of Chinese artifacts in the world, and the Science Centre, which my nine-year-old, exceptionally intelligent grandson claims to be one of the seven wonders of the world.

As professionals, architects are quite different from any others. They are educated in a school where criticism of the most devastating kind is part of the system, and they frequently put their all — money, time and talent — into competitions for public and other buildings where only one is chosen.

In general, they are a most likeable and dedicated bunch and, if Toronto is the great place I think it is for living, working and playing, the architects in large part have made it so.

St. Lawrence and Old York

BY RON THOM

In the days when the buildings on Front Street dabbled their toes in the waters of Lake Ontario, the south-east corner of Toronto — then the town of York — was the mercantile heart of the city. When disastrous fires destroyed the early buildings in the 19th century, they were replaced by fine new brick buildings. Today, many have disappeared although some survivors have found a new place in the life of the city. Few of these lay claim to great architecture, but all express most eloquently the history of the city, its people, their attitudes, postures and ethics.

Tour 1

A tour of the historic old part of Toronto logically divides in two parts — west and east of Jarvis.

The western tour begins on King Street just east of Yonge Street at St. James' Cathedral. This studious reproduction of a 14th-century English Gothic cathedral, by architects Thomas Ridout and F.W. Cumberland, belongs to the oldest parish in Toronto and is the official seat of the Bishop of Toronto. It is the third St. James' on the site and was opened in 1853. The original wooden building was constructed by pioneers and soldiers in 1803.

The steeple is interesting. It was not completed until 20 years after the opening of the church and, at 324 feet, is the tallest steeple in Canada. The illuminated spire clock, for many years officially used to guide ships into the harbor, was a present from the city in 1875. The city still maintains this clock.

The park surrounding the Cathedral used to be the churchyard. Many of the old headstones have been set into the porch walls and make fascinating reading.

Walking across the park on the east side of the Cathedral, towards Jarvis Street, to the north you can see Tom Taylor's store, the modern day version of old York ships' chandlers. Instead of the sailing ships of the West Indies trading fleet it outfits the recreational sailor. To its left is the lush jungle of Mr. Greenjeans' plant warehouse and restaurant.

It seems to many who work in this area that the demolition-parking-lot-new-office-block cycle has been going ahead unchecked. But there have been individuals who have opted for regeneration. Grumbles Coffee House on Jarvis started the movement and its owners went on to renovate a pleasant pub up the street, the Jarvis House. Grumbles was quickly followed by Salmagundi, with its tremendous variety of bric-a-brac both ancient and

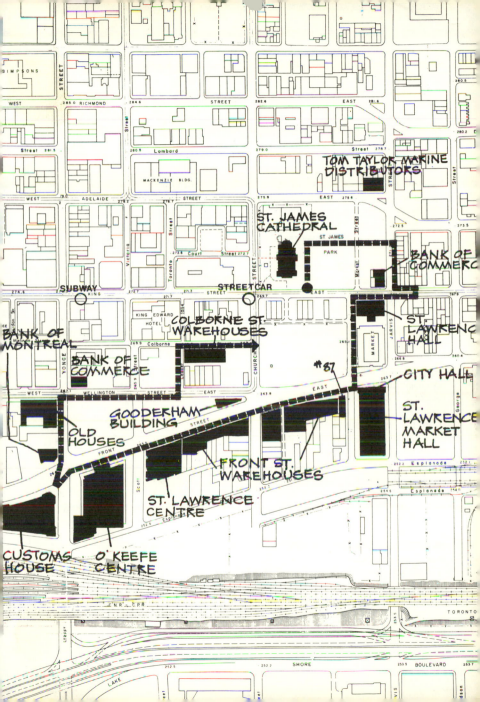

modern; and around the corner on King Street, Renaissance, which as its name implies, gives a new life to the artifacts of preceding generations. Grumbles, since closed, is now recycled as a charming French crêpe house, Le Papillon.

On the north-west corner of King and Jarvis is the market branch of the Canadian Imperial Bank of Commerce (originally the Bank of British North America). You can still see where the words "Market Branch" have been removed from the architrave.

One of Toronto's finest 19th-century buildings, St. Lawrence Hall, is on the opposite corner. It was designed by William Thomas in true Renaissance tradition. Its fine stone carving is a rarity in Toronto. Look up at the feathers, swords and bugles, and at the cast iron balconies. Built during the prosperity of the 1850s as a public hall together with a covered market at the rear, St. Lawrence Hall was the scene of every noteworthy social event for many years: from performances by Jenny Lind, military balls and government receptions to temperance meetings, anti-slavery meetings and public lectures. It gradually slipped down the social scale through a velocipede school to a doss house for the unemployed. Rescued by the City of Toronto, it was restored to its former elegance and purpose in 1967 as a centennial project.

Walking down the west side of the building, past today's dismal substitute for the original covered market, you come face to face with Toronto's first City Hall. It has been part of the St. Lawrence Market since 1890 when a second city hall was built and is now visible since the Market's recent renovation. Not everyone approved of this structure when it was erected in 1844 at a cost of $52,000. One Mercer Adam commented "this is a very strange building, and it was unfortunate for the reputation of the architect (Henry Bower Lane) that he had not left the province before he completed the building, instead of afterwards."

If you walk through the central entrance into the market, then turn and look back, you will see the very fine south side or rear of the original building. The doorway to the right of the entrance leads to the stairway to the great hall.

87 Front Street East, next door to the market has been part of the commercial scene in this area since the mid-1860s. The building has been renovated and restored as a provincial liquor outlet with an extensive rare wine department downstairs.

For another change of pace, check the delightful Aggregation Gallery, then enjoy the dazzling display of Scandinavian designs in Karelia Studio in the same block.

It will not come as a surprise that the curious building in isolation between Front and Wellington Streets is known as the "flat iron" building. It was built in 1892 for Gooderham's, the distillery people, and designed by architect William Kaufman.

The buildings on the south side of Front Street are good examples of the factories and warehouses built on the

Flat iron building

waterfront when the harbor came up to the Esplanade. They are wood and iron post and beam construction with well organized and sometimes elaborate masonry facades.

Fifty years ago Toronto had more than 100 theatres, vaudeville and burlesque houses. Two successors to this tradition are the St. Lawrence Centre for the Performing Arts and the O'Keefe Centre.

The St. Lawrence Centre, a city centennial project completed in 1970, was designed by Gordon S. Adamson & Associates. It is divided into two parts, an 831-seat theatre and a 483-seat town hall. The Town Hall's programs are usually co-operative ventures between the Centre and community sponsors. From October to April, the Theatre is used by the resident repertory company; the rest of the year it accommodates visiting theatre, opera and dance groups.

The 3,220-seat O'Keefe Centre, next door, was built by the O'Keefe Brewery in 1960 but later taken over by the City. Architects were Page and Steele and Earle C. Morgan.

Beyond O'Keefe on the south-west corner of Yonge and Front is the Customs House, built in 1876 and still fulfilling its early role. On the opposite corner is the site of Toronto's first Bank of Montreal, built in 1845. The present building by Darling and Curry was built in 1885. Holbrooke and Millington were the sculptors. Unfortunately some of the charm has been lost in recent insensitive improvements.

The Bank of Montreal at the corner of Front and Yonge Streets

Another bank of this period, by Henry Langley, the Canadian Imperial Bank of Commerce, stands on the north-east corner of Yonge and Wellington Streets. From this corner also is a fine view of the baroque detailing on the facades of early houses on the west side of Yonge and the south side of Wellington.

Retracing your steps along Wellington Street to Leader Lane, go north to Colborne Street and another example of the old warehouses built in the 1880s. Occupants of the street joined together to purchase 45 to 51 Colborne and rebuilt the interior as contemporary office space, restoring the fine brick and stone facade.

To wind up this tour, try one of the many and varied restaurants in the immediate neighborhood from the Cafe du Marché on Colborne, to Les Copains and Graf Bobby on Wellington and the Old Fish Market opposite St. Lawrence Market. On the Esplanade are Brandy's, The Organ Grinder, and the Old Spaghetti Factory, with the Muddy York around the corner on Church Street. Or on a fine day, you can picnic in the park around the Cathedral with a sandwich from Pasquale's on King Street.

Tour 2

On the way to the corner of King and Berkeley where this tour begins, pause at King and Sherbourne where there are a couple of interesting places to visit. On King, the "Storeroom" has a very good selection of posters, framed and unframed, and many well chosen handicrafts. At 37 Sherbourne the third generation of B.B. Smith's carry on one of the most interesting fur businesses in town — the slogan is "from trapper to wearer." As you walk in you are assailed by the pungent smell of tanning. Mika Interior Designs and Marenco, Inc. share space at 234 King Street East. At 300 King East is Klaus Nienkamper's store which stocks some of the best contemporary furniture from France, Italy, Sweden and Switzerland. This building dates from 1878 and used to be Mr. J.H. Greenshield's general store serving both the farmers who came to the St. Lawrence market and the carriage trade. This area is fast becoming a theatre centre, with Second City Revue on Lombard Street, Factory Theatre Lab on Adelaide, and the Toronto Free Theatre on Berkeley.

Also on Berkeley Street is the former No. 4 Firehall which is now the "Firehall Theatre", and home of Canada's oldest theatrical company — the University Alumnae Dramatic Club. The firehall, the second on the site, was built in 1900. It was saved from demolition by the Dramatic Club in 1972. The now slightly stubby hose tower unfortunately has lost its fanciful wooden bell enclosure and decorated window heads, but otherwise the sturdy building remains intact. Peek inside to see the intimate 154-seat, end-stage auditorium and the studio workshop theatre on the third floor in the former billiards room.

Across the street is a group of early Toronto workmen's cottages which architect Joan Burt has turned into architects' and interior designers' offices and showrooms.

Further along King, past Parliament Street, you will come to the city's

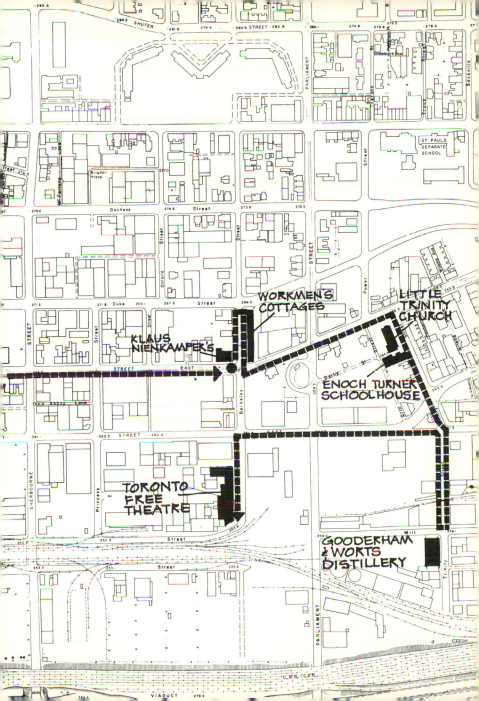

WORKMEN'S COTTAGES

LITTLE TRINITY CHURCH

KLAUS NIENKAMPER'S

ENOCH TURNER SCHOOLHOUSE

TORONTO FREE THEATRE

GOODERHAM & WORTS DISTILLERY

ST PAULS SEPARATE SCHOOL

oldest surviving church, Little Trinity Church. The Protestant Irish poor of the city didn't feel too comfortable with either the atmosphere or the high pew rents at St. James' Cathedral, so Little Trinity was founded in 1842 to meet their needs. The architect was the same Henry Lane of City Hall fame (Tour 1). In 1961 the church was badly damaged by fire, but funds were raised to restore the church and today it draws a congregation from all over Metro Toronto.

To the south of the church is Toronto's oldest school building. Free education for the poor was a very controversial issue in Toronto in the mid 19th century. When the aldermen, in spite of the Common Schools' Act, closed the common schools for a year as a waste of money, Enoch Turner, an Englishman from Staffordshire built his school. It was completed in 1848 with room for 240 children and writing desks for 80. It was saved a few years ago from demolition and restored by concerned groups. Now children come from schools all over the city for classes in living history, and the hall is available for business meetings and social events.

The restoration of the church and schoolhouse has given new stimulus to this area. An attractive interior design studio — d'Lesing Interiors — has courageously opened on the north side of King, opposite the church, and hopefully more of that side of the street will soon be converted.

The Gooderham and Worts distillery has been at the end of Trinity Street since 1832, and is an excellent example of the high standard of design used in industrial buildings of the 19th century. There are approximately 46 buildings in the complex, most of them dating back to the 1860s and '70s — only three date as late as the 1920s.

The grey stone building on the south-west corner is on the site of the original windmill where William Gooderham and his nephew James Worts initially ground grain at the edge of the lake, before gradually switching over entirely to the profitable business of distilling. It was built in 1861 of Kingston limestone, the walls three feet thick.

Walking west on Front Street you come to another fine group of 19th century industrial buildings stretching from Berkeley down to the Esplanade. The five-building complex, next to "Dalton's (1834) Maraschino and Glace Cherries, Mustard" establishment, was put in the wreckers' hands in 1970. But instead of tearing down the derelict building, the Greenspoon Brothers fell in love with them and bought them. The gasworks, where once artificial gas was made from coal, now houses the head office of the wreckers and after sandblasting the Toronto Knitting and Yarn Factory (J. Simpson, Prop. 1880), they loaned it to the Toronto Free Theatre. This company produces original Canadian plays for an audience that includes flower children and Rosedale matrons — no longer for free, alas.

Top: Enoch Turner Schoolhouse since renovation. Built in 1848
Bottom: Gooderham & Worts Distillery

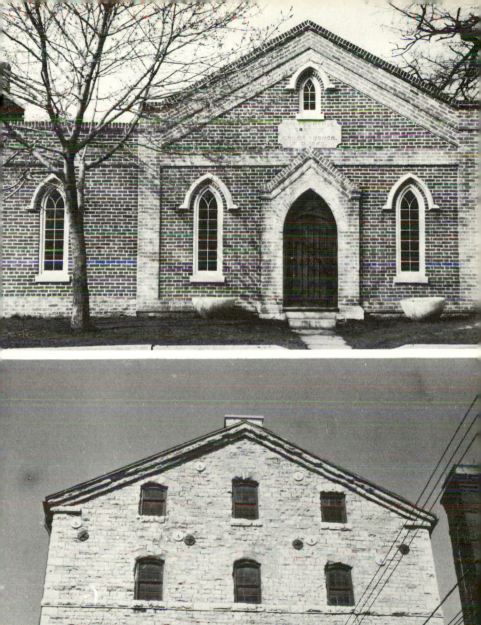

The Downtown Core

BY ERLAND GUSTAVS

Tour One

Yonge Street, wrote an observer a hundred years ago, "is the main artery of the city's life ... All day its sidewalks are thronged by visitors eagerly intent on business or pleasure; by night illuminated by the brilliance of electric light, the scene is hardly less animated."

Almost the exact words apply today. However, instead of promenading Victorians, lower Yonge Street is filled with shopping homemakers from suburbia; mothers from the subsidized housing beyond Jarvis Street with two or three children in tow; secretaries in the latest styles; and young hopefuls with blue suits and mod haircuts from the financial district. In the evening, as stores close, the crowd (a slightly different one) shifts with the action a few blocks north to the bars, strip joints and "blue" movie houses above Queen.

This is a good place to start a walking tour of downtown because the cheap cheer of the old east side of Yonge contrasts wildly with the modern new Eaton Centre opposite.

For years Eaton's was located farther south, slap across Queen Street from its rival, Simpsons. Although the new Centre is located two long blocks north, the old rivals still relate to and compete with each other because the distance between them has been cleverly used to create a shopping mall, The Galleria.

And no mean mall it is. It's a spectacular new downtown indoor space, several stories high, topped by glass. It has such appeal that even Birk's, the jewellers whose blue boxes have been known to Canadian bluebloods for years, was persuaded to move its main store off Yonge Street and onto the new internal street.

It is indeed a street, a *new* Toronto street, not simply Yonge Street relocated. This one offers shoppers and strollers warmth in winter, cool comfort in summer and, because of its scale, narrowness, and absence of automobiles, the mood of a market street from another era. However, the elevators rising to hidden parking garages above, the escalators carrying shoppers silently between levels, and the prices displayed soon remind you that this is still Toronto and this is still now.

Yet even here you can step back in time by turning out of the spectacular Galleria at the exit marked "Trinity Square." There, unexpectedly, dwarfed by the mass of its new neighbor, is Toronto's famous and beloved Holy Trinity church. When Eaton Centre was in the planning stage, the public insisted that the

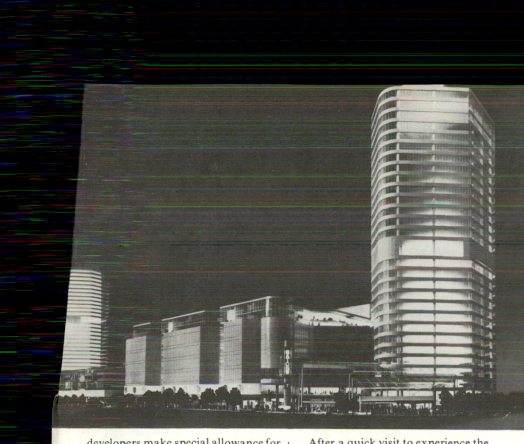

developers make special allowance for Trinity, even demanding that the sun be allowed — literally — to continue to shine on the church whose slim twin towers have been city landmarks for many years.

When it was consecrated in 1847, Holy Trinity gazed south across a swampy area draining into Taddle Creek. To the north: forest. Funds to build the church were donated by an anonymous English lady who had never been to Toronto. The deed stipulated that no rentals could be charged for seating.

The church does not sit alone in its new square. Its longtime neighbors remain: number six, built to house church activities; and number ten, built in 1861 for the rector, the illustrious Dr. Scadding, author of *Toronto of Old*.

After a quick visit to experience the "greenhouse" entrance lobby to the Centre at the corner of Dundas and Yonge, and to notice the mezzanine restaurant with its bustling view of people heading in and out of Dundas subway station, turn east on Dundas to Bond Street. At 82, flickering gaslight welcomes the stroller to the Toronto Historical Board's carefully restored showpiece — the last house of William Lyon Mackenzie, newspaper publisher, government critic, "rabid reformer", and first mayor of Toronto. The house was a present to him by friends in 1859, and he lived here until his death.

This house was originally one of a

Above: The New Eaton Centre

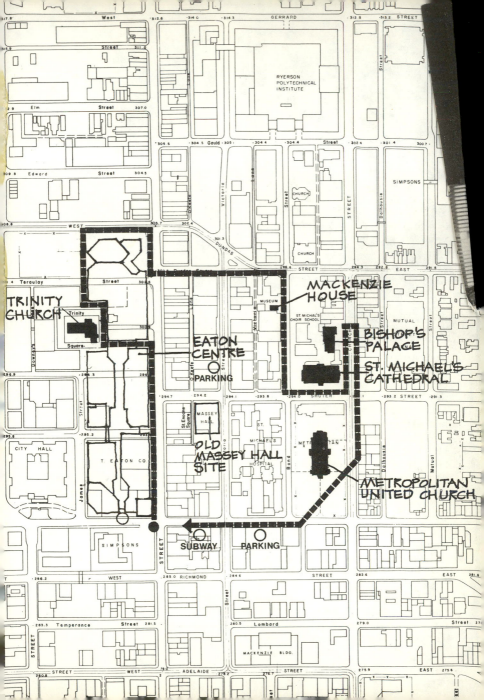

Toronto's ever changing skyline viewed across Nathan Phillips Square

series of identical, attached, terraced houses that stretched along this block. As late as 1875, Toronto was rich in treed squares lined with similar well-designed, detached or row houses. The scale was low and well-related to people, and the streets provided a sense of comfort and security. Unfortunately little of this remains, the milieu was destroyed by the Toronto building boom of the second half of the 19th century.

Walking south now, you may hear choir voices. The singing comes from either St. Michael's Cathedral or the Metropolitan United Church. Even today they're handsome structures, but think how these church spires must have dominated Toronto's skyline when the scale of buildings was low.

When it was built in 1845, St. Michael's had a large landscaped square to the south but over the years the Cathedral has been squeezed in by buildings and streets. The main body of the church was built in grey brick and stone. Spire and dormers, built later, were designed by a different firm of architects. The interior of the church and the Bishop's Palace built at the same time on Church Street, show a mastery of detailing.

The Metropolitan United Church, south of Shuter Street, has an unusually generous space around it for a downtown church. You can rest here on the grass, or picnic at one of the many tables. The yellow brick Gothic church was built in 1872 and seats 2,200. Seriously damaged in a 1928 fire, it is now restored almost to its

original design although its original patterned roof has been replaced by plain black.

On the opposite side of Church Street are many of Toronto's pawn shops, small loan shops, and clothing exchanges announcing the blighted but improving area to the east. (Restoration projects underway here warrant further exploration on your own.) As you turn back toward Yonge, you see yet another sign that Torontonians care about their city: all along Queen Street are freshly-planted trees.

Tour Two

The Business District

This second downtown walking tour begins in Nathan Phillips Square, the front yard of our New City Hall. A good place to pause before walking. The square is easily accessible by subway to Queen Street or Osgoode, or, if you come by car, you can park in the garage under the square.

The view from the square offers a capsule preview of the tour to come and also a sense of Toronto's past. The towers of the commercial and financial centre are framed by the Old City Hall to the east and Osgoode Hall to the west.

Don't let the cast-iron fence fool you. Osgoode's grounds *are* open to the public. The ornate fence was originally built to keep cows and horses off the manicured lawns. Such fences, functional as well as decorative, were numerous in early Toronto. The building, containing government offices, legal offices and accommodation for law students, was originally erected in three stages starting in 1829, and has since been altered and added to. It was named after The Honorable William Osgoode who was the first Chief Justice of Upper Canada (1792-1794). Although trials are mostly held in the New Metro Court House just to the north, appeals to the Supreme Court of Ontario are heard in this historic building. Visitors are welcome to take conducted tours to see the splendor of Osgoode's grand staircase and the rotunda and, with the permission of the librarian, the Great Library — a truly magnificent room.

Facing New City Hall is the huge (1,450 rooms) Sheraton Centre Hotel which boasts Canada's longest bar, a shopping concourse, and a garden court complete with waterfall. All this is open to the public.

Near here, connected by the fast-growing network of underground walkways, are the Richmond-Adelaide Centre — its shopping mall includes a liquor store, boutiques, a sensational continental pastry shop, and a restaurant under a greenhouse roof — and the York Centre.

King Street, originally named Duke Street, has come a long way since it was York's first street laid out in 1793 by Governor Simcoe. It was then the northern boundary of the new town. Today, King and Bay marks the very centre of Canada's financial world. More people carry attaché cases here than anywhere else in the city, and Lincolns and Cadillacs haughtily await VIPs from the banks, while chauffeurs smoke and laugh quietly together.

The Toronto-Dominion Centre on King was the first of Toronto's superdevelopments. The separate single-storey banking pavilion is one of the great Mies van der Rohe's designs. Mies was involved in the entire project as a consultant, and the towers and the pavilion show the simplicity and attention to detail expected from this master architect. Visitors can admire the view of Toronto Island and the lake from the observation gallery or from the Fifty-fourth, a pricey top-floor restaurant.

Farther south on Bay Street, the Royal Bank's two triangular gold towers face each other, enclosing between them spectacular multi-storey space. And yes, it *is* real gold that humbly tints those windows. North on Bay, you can stop in at the busy Toronto Stock Exchange. On weekdays, they offer you a fascinating guided tour.

The owners of Commerce Court, east of the Toronto-Dominion Centre, at King and Bay, are to be commended for their decision to incorporate the existing 34-storey headquarters building, erected in 1931 (as the tallest building in the British Commonwealth), into the shiny new complex. Functionally, the old tower has been entirely modernized; but the exterior and ground floor interior have been restored. Visit the main floor great hall and experience the gilded splendor of a bank in the early 1930s.

Before walking up Bay Street (called Bear Street when it was the western boundary of the town of York) to the Old City Hall, note the Bank of Montreal's new skyscraper, clad grandly in Italian marble. At 85

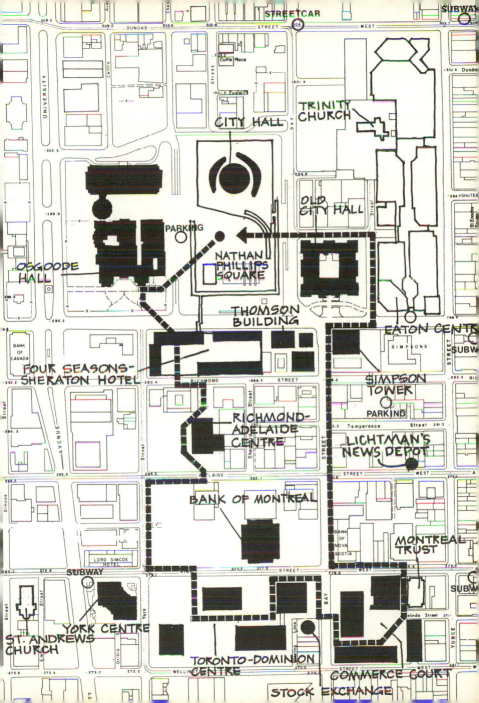

stories, it's the current winner in the highest-building-in-Canada sweepstakes (if you don't count Toronto's CN Tower, which, of course, tops the world).

Facing both city halls on Queen is the North American capital of the empire of Lord Thomson of Fleet, the Canadian who became the world's most successful newspaper magnate.

The Old City Hall, massive, castle-like, dominating its surroundings, was designed in 1890 by the winner of an international competition. Note the lavish exterior decorations — carved figures, geometric and floral shapes.

Northeast of Old City Hall is the Salvation Army's national headquarters. The organization has owned the site since 1885 and, when its new brick-faced building was completed in 1954, it was a unique addition to downtown architecture.

Facing Old City Hall is the Simpsons Tower, owned by the department store that stretches along Queen Street to Yonge. Simpsons opened at Queen and Yonge in 1895: the tower and the portion below were added in 1969. The original store consists of the seven structural "bays" west from Yonge and Queen and the five bays south. It is designed in the Romanesque style that was fashionable at the time. Simpsons' decision to restore its exterior is welcome in a city that has learned to appreciate its past. The recycled building can offer a dramatic contrast with the new Eaton's and the two buildings together bracket a time span of nearly 100 years in an instant convincing demonstration of Toronto's past and future.

Cut back now behind Old City Hall, across Bay Street and under the elevated walkway to stand again before the New City Hall.

Like its predecessor, the New City Hall was the result of an international architectural competition which attracted more entries than any such competition ever had before. From 520 submissions, an international jury selected the project submitted by Viljo Revell of Helsinki. It becomes difficult to remember the controversy that once raged over this architecture and the "modernistic" Henry Moore sculpture. Tours of the New City Hall run every half hour.

The square that stretches before the building is named after the Toronto mayor who initiated this project Nathan Phillips can be proud, because this mighty square is today the heart of the city.

Top left: Commerce Court
Top right: T-D Centre
Bottom left: Interior view of City Hall's pod
Bottom right: Metro Court House

The Toronto Islands

BY ROGER DU TOIT

Other cities have island parks. There are other island communities. Other neighborhoods are pedestrian sanctuaries. There are other examples of high-density but low-rise single family housing. Other communities have a strong identity and support their own newspapers, day schools and community centres. There are other homes built on publicly-owned leased lots. But as far as I know, the Toronto Islands are unique in combining these characteristics — and right next to the core of the city.

The Toronto Islands are a group of small islands, some virtually joined, others linked by bridges, so you can walk or ride a bike from one end to the other. Four miles long and seldom wider than 500 feet, the sand bar which forms them was created by centuries of wave action scouring away an ancient promontory at Scarborough, leaving the present bluffs, and redepositing it where the Islands are now. Early maps tell a story of continuously shifting sands and even today the Toronto Harbour Commission has to draw a new map every year.

At the turn of the century, about half of the Islands' present 750 acres was parkland, some of it left wild. The rest was a mixture of residential accommodation — from hotels and expensive summer houses to tents. The summer population rose to almost 8,000. They lived in communities clustered in three areas (corresponding to the present ferry stops): Hanlan's Point, Centre Island, and Ward's Island. Today Algonquin and Ward's are the only islands which still have homes — some 260 of them. These are also the most interesting and least crowded islands to visit.

Getting there, as the cliché says, is half the fun. You go by ferry. The dock is between the foot of Bay and Yonge Streets. The fare is minimal. Phone 367-8193 for ferry times because the schedule changes throughout the year. Parking costs $2. On summer weekends avoid mid-day like the plague. Not only will you not be able to park, but it could take hours to get through the line-ups to the boat. The Islands are also beautiful in the winter but dress for the biting wind.

Take the Ward's Island boat, which is always less crowded. On the trip across the bay, turn back and watch the city slip into profile — it seems to grow more beautiful the farther away you get!

As you approach the Ward's dock (about 8 min.), watch for the Queen City Yacht Club to the west. This is a club for working sailors where motor boats are scorned. In summer, boats

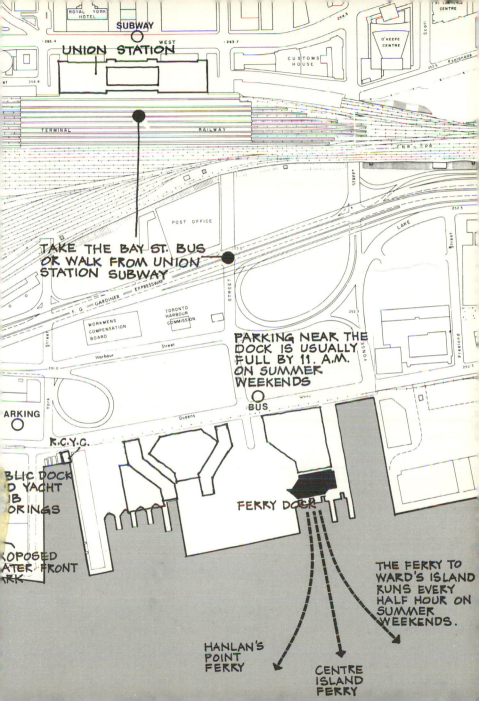

SUBWAY

UNION STATION

ROYAL YORK HOTEL

WEST

CUSTOMS HOUSE

O'KEEFE CENTRE

TERMINAL RAILWAY

POST OFFICE

TAKE THE BAY ST. BUS OR WALK FROM UNION STATION SUBWAY

F. G. GARDINER EXPRESSWAY

WORKMENS COMPENSATION BOARD

TORONTO HARBOUR COMMISSION

PARKING NEAR THE DOCK IS USUALLY FULL BY 11 A.M. ON SUMMER WEEKENDS

Harbour Street

BUS

PARKING

Queens Quay

R.C.Y.C.

BLIC DOCK D YACHT JB ORINGS

FERRY DOCK

PROPOSED ATER FRONT RK

THE FERRY TO WARD'S ISLAND RUNS EVERY HALF HOUR ON SUMMER WEEKENDS.

HANLAN'S POINT FERRY

CENTRE ISLAND FERRY

Clockwise from the left: The William Inglis ferry at Ward's Dock, Centre Island Children's Farm, ducks in the park, The Gibraltar Point Lighthouse.

of all descriptions are moored along both sides of the lagoon which separates Ward's from the adjacent Algonquin Island.

The old Ward's village green directly ahead of the ferry dock is now only a shadow of what it was in its hey-day, when it was flanked with hotels and shops. But the "village green" tradition persists with baseball, lawn bowling and tennis — plus the occasional bake sale, children's fancy dress parade, or other community celebration.

In winter, the lagoons become an extended skating rink, where the adventurous can travel for miles around the Islands. You are liable to meet an ice boat, manned by a ruddy-faced year-round sailor. In mid-winter, the Islanders hold an ice carnival. It's farther west near the bridge, with balloons, races, and hot chili con carne.

Ward's Island is perfect for cross-country skiing, too. And if you get cold, wet, or hungry, you can drop into one of two "Open Houses" arranged by Island residents every winter weekend. Signs giving the addresses are posted at the dock and bridge.

The Ward's Island community consists of about 120 small wooden cottages packed tightly on lots originally laid out for tents. In fact, many of the present houses started out as clusters of sheds around a tent which eventually was replaced with a permanent roof. In the absence of strict bylaws, an attitude of add-or-change-as-the-mood-seizes still continues, drawing many free spirits to the Island. The houses, while detached,

are so close together they seem to foster great neighborliness. On some full-moon summer nights, the streets become a kind of communal living room with the surrounding houses used as coat-rooms, washrooms, and places to prepare food and drink for a "come-one, come-all" street party.

The streets and avenues are really no more than paved footpaths. One, called Lakeshore Avenue, leads to the quay of the Eastern Gap, still equipped with long-disused cast-iron bollards. On the way is an abandoned ice house in a wilderness inhabited by numerous rabbits and an occasional pheasant. Across the gap is Cherry Beach, reached from the mainland by the relatively few people who know it. Both sides of the gap lure fishermen — particularly for the spring smelt run.

The Harbour Commission's landfill headland can also be seen from here. It marks the beginning of a once-proposed harbour expansion, more recently a proposed aquatic park, but for now, a wild life refuge.

From the south end of the quay is a startling and unforgettable view of Toronto's downtown skyscrapers, seen through a rustic foreground.

Ward's Beach, which runs west from the gap, is the best and least crowded on the Islands. Facing it are several cottages whose scrubby gardens, in a running fight with wind and sand, recall Cape Cod or Martha's Vineyard. These cottages mark the beginning of a classic (but renewed) boardwalk. It was once flanked by many large and elegant mansions. This boardwalk is a popular promenade and bicycle path on a sunny day, whatever the season. In winter it offers the excitement of a storm at sea, with huge waves crashing over the breakwater.

Only two houses remain on the boardwalk; a former rectory, now used as a senior citizens' centre, and a bungalow occupied by the park's superintendent. The sites of the rest are now forlornly empty save for a few overgrown foundation walls, pathways and shrubberies. There are also some little-used picnic tables; the crowd is a mile away at Centre Island.

A wood humpbacked bridge is the only way to Algonquin Island. It has also blocked expansion of berth facilities of Queen City Yacht Club, leaving the rest of the lagoon free for other, more informal users. It's first come, first served — build your own dock and berth your boat — the only marina in Toronto where squatters' rights prevail.

Many of the cottages around the perimeter of Algonquin Island are examples of an original Island vernacular. They were floated over from the long-gone Hanlan's Point community, when it was cleared for the present airport. They have a picturebook charm. Their central front doors are flanked by windows and battered "skirts" slope outward from windowsills to the ground. The pitched roofs are broken by mansard windows, lighting ideal studio space in the lofts. Many do in fact contain studios, because architects, painters, sculptors, potters and home crafters abound on the Islands.

Despite the fact that Islanders could be forced to vacate at any time, many houses have been recently renovated in a home-made sort of way. Such efforts are boosted by a lively community association. Two of the latest major improvements are a shingle-clad geodesic dome perched atop a roof on Dacotah Avenue. The other is a cedar addition on Nottawa Avenue. The owner of the latter even requested a building permit — an event so unusual on the Island that it required the approval of the full session of the Metro Council.

It's worth walking along Seneca Avenue at sunset or after dark for what is perhaps the finest view of Toronto in the entire city. There's also a view across the bay of the stately mansion, jetty and outbuildings of the Royal Canadian Yacht Club. Its atmosphere of leisured establishment is reminiscent of a grander era. The club is approached by water by an ancient river boat. This boat, by the way, is said to be the oldest in the world on Lloyd's register. Another way in — for members only — is via a private bridge off the lagoon road, which connects Ward's with Centre Island.

Continue your walk to Centre past the Islands' two churches. Both are wood construction: the Catholic one is brown; the Anglican, St. Andrew's-by-the-Lake, is white clapboard. It was built in 1889 and moved to its present site in 1956. Both congregations have dwindled drastically in recent years, but the churches are popular for weddings, baptisms and midnight masses that are community events on the Islands. One of the most delightful weddings involved a grand ride by bride and groom from the church to the ferry dock amid piles of blossoms in a pony gig. The couple

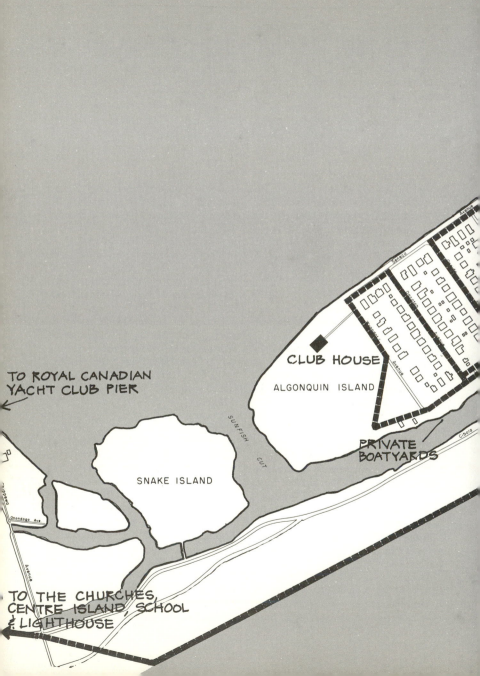

TO ROYAL CANADIAN
YACHT CLUB PIER

CLUB HOUSE

ALGONQUIN ISLAND

SUNFISH CUT

SNAKE ISLAND

PRIVATE
BOATYARDS

Cibola

Seneca

Wyandot Avenue

Avenue

Onondaga Ave

Avenue

TO THE CHURCHES,
CENTRE ISLAND, SCHOOL
& LIGHTHOUSE

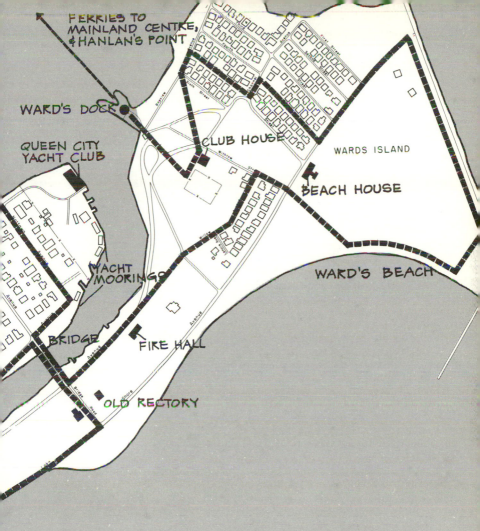

FERRIES TO MAINLAND CENTRE, & HANLAN'S POINT

WARD'S DOCK

QUEEN CITY YACHT CLUB

CLUB HOUSE

WARDS ISLAND

BEACH HOUSE

YACHT MOORINGS

WARD'S BEACH

BRIDGE

FIRE HALL

OLD RECTORY

were followed by formally attired guests — on bicycles.

Centre Island is the park's main entertainment area. There's a farm-yard complete with barn, paddocks and chicken coops; boat rentals; miniature amusement village with a train circuit running through the Island's only hill (artificial and providing great sport for skiers during the winter); a puppet theatre; bicycle rentals, and more.

Formal gardens are laid out where the "main drag" was when Centre Island was a live community with as many residents as it now receives visitors. On the axis of these gardens is what looks like the beginning of a bridge to Niagara Falls but is only a lookout to the lake.

Beyond this is the school and water filtration plant. The school, besides serving the Island children, doubles as a nature study centre. Children from all over Toronto come here to live and study for a week at a time. There is a bird sanctuary and nature reserve behind the filtration plant, and the school itself has a museum of natural history.

The oldest structure on the Island is nearby — Gibraltar Point Lighthouse. It stands on what was once the tip of the original sand bar but is now too far inland to be operative. The lighthouse has its own ghost. There are several versions of the story — they tell of soldiers demanding beer, an old murder, and a skeleton in the sand.

Centre Island is rich in such nostalgia to those who know its history. Even if you don't you'll find it a great place to spend a day.

The downtown Toronto skyline

The Beaches

BY JACK KLEIN ASSISTED BY
TED WOOD AND JAMES SMITH

When I was in high school in Toronto there was a style of dancing called "The Balmy." As I recall, it was a rather slow step not demanding of expertise with rather a lot of body contact. It was considered a little risqué and daring. We all knew it evolved in a distinctive and identifiable but remote part of the city — Balmy Beach, or the Beaches.

The Beaches has somehow always retained this slightly remote and distinctive quality while being very close to the centre of the city. This is largely due to its isolation — by the Greenwood Race Track on the west and to a lesser extent the Water Works on the east. The northern limit is Queen Street, which also is "main street" both in style and character. The greatest attraction is the lakefront — continuous and public for its entire length between the race track and the Water Works.

This small precinct has become a very desirable and highly sought-after area in which to live. It probably has more acres of park per person than any other residential area in Toronto and, extraordinarily, more than a mile of unpolluted sand beach. While it has been largely populated by Anglo-Saxons, this is beginning to change. A great variety of people of reasonable economic diversity now live here.

At the end of the 1800s, the Beaches was a suburban cottage district like Long Branch and Mimico to the west. Before World War I it even had its own small amusement park. As the city grew, cottages gave way to permanent year-round homes, although a few cottage-like houses still exist. Identified with the area have been a succession of successful football players, hockey stars, writers, and pianist Glen Gould.

Despite the growth of Metro some twenty miles beyond the Beaches to the east, Toronto's public transportation system has always used the area as a terminus. Before 1920, the Toronto Street Railway Company ran a jitney trolley along the Queen Street line. A more efficient but less nostalgic service is now offered by the TTC whose Queen cars will deliver you to the Water Works.

First on a walking tour of The Beaches is the Water Works itself. You may want to take a conducted tour through, although from the point of view of architecture or general interest, it isn't very exciting — unless you are hopelessly addicted to potable water. The buildings are disasters both

One of the cottages that lingered on

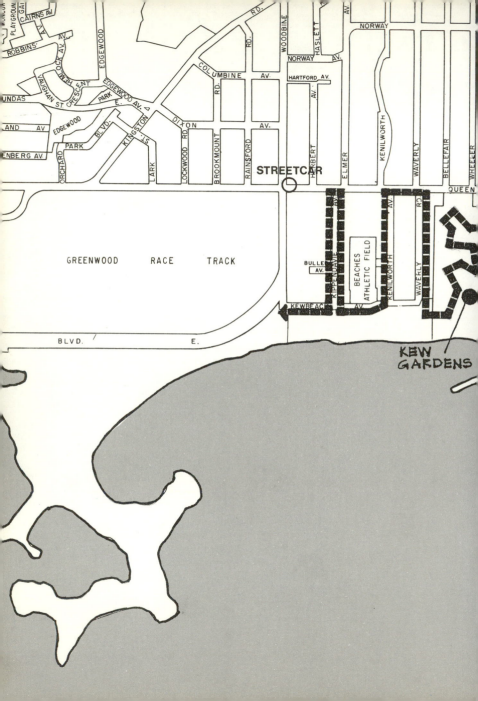

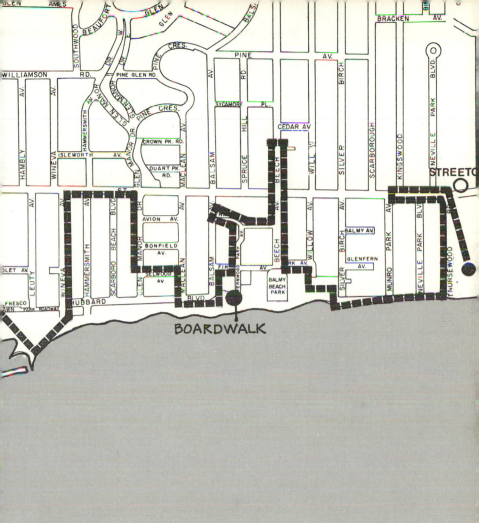

BOARDWALK

inside and out, and there is not even the end-of-tour enticement that a candy factory or brewery can offer. The Water Works' park-like setting is likely to be more fun — a great open space for walkers and kite fliers.

On the north side of Queen Street, directly across the road from the Water Works, are a pair of walk-up apartments designed by architect Michael Bach. They seem strange in Toronto. Their scale is odd and the style is reminiscent of 1950 Swiss or Scandinavian but they are pleasantly sited on a neatly landscaped yard.

To get the first direct contact with the lake, walk down Nursewood Road from the Water Works. At the bottom of Nursewood there is a small and very clean, orderly apartment building by Tampold and Wells, Architects. Its occupants are very fortunate. From their balconies, they have a sweeping view of the lake.

From this point, any westerly route (towards the city skyline) is interesting. The one suggested on the map offers some visual highlights.

For the first three blocks, the beach runs from the water right up to private houses. A very convenient and picturesque boardwalk, now in need of some repair, starts at Silverbirch Avenue. You can follow it the full length of the rest of the Beaches area. It is inevitable that you will come to envy those lucky few who live in a group of houses right on the boardwalk between Glen Manor Drive and Wineva Avenue. If you should take this walk on a fine Sunday morning the boardwalk will be literally jammed with walkers, dogs running in and out, babies in carriages, bicycles on the special (however badly maintained) paths provided for them, and others just sitting on the occasional bench enjoying the air and view. A refreshment stand beside the boardwalk at Kew Gardens offers standard concession fare of hot dogs, popcorn, and pop — but even this tastes good in the open air.

In the evening, just before it gets dark, a walk along the beach is quiet and restful. Except in winter, a few late sailors and the inevitable canoeist go by silently just offshore. The lights of freighters farther out wink in the dusk.

The streets between the lake and Queen Street are sometimes exceptional. Queen itself has a small town quality. There is a great mixture of boutiques, meat markets, health food stores, and antique shops. The views from Queen down some of the streets are surprisingly inviting. Try some.

This is one district which will not tempt walkers who would like to refresh themselves with an interesting meal. There are enough eateries to sustain life, but if good food is required — eat before or after your visit here. For the desperate, there are a few modest snack places for coffee and a sandwich or fish and chips. Or maybe you could plan a picnic on the beach.

Many houses are worth searching out. Watch for houses finished in wood shingles, reminiscent of the shingle houses of Newport, R.I. Some fine shapes and forms. The rows of elegant fourplexes on Hammersmith Avenue are specially stately. Particularly watch for delightful whimsical places like the Blarney Castle on Lee Avenue. Look for an improbable vertical pile-up of rooms at the second house east of Silverbirch facing the lake.

The west end of the Beaches ends at a public swimming pool by architects Wilson and Newton — a handsome, strong structure. You can swim here free or from here catch the streetcar back to the city, pretending all the while that you are only going back to your job and can come back that evening.

The Beaches, unfortunately, is under some pressure for redevelopment. It would be a pity if this occurred in a way which changed or altered its essential character. The quality of the scale is especially important — the rather narrow streets, the charming vistas. Every bit of space is accounted for: either it is public like the beach or the parks, or it is territorially identified as private. High density, high-rise apartments could quickly destroy all this.

A stately old home

Kensington

BY JEROME MARKSON AND
ANDREW CLARKE

In the 1870's the area we now call Kensington was parcelled into suburban lots and the streets that became home for middle class Anglo-Saxons were given elegant British names such as Kensington Avenue, Fitzroy Terrace, Oxford, Wales and Baldwin. For thirty years streets were kept tidy, lawns kept manicured, and the eventual conversion of the neighborhood into a street market could not have seemed less likely.

The first signs of tranquil Kensington becoming a hive of commerce came after 1905 when Russian, Polish and Jewish immigrants came from east of Spadina. Because these people had been excluded from the Anglo-Saxon business community they opened stalls in front of their houses and sold goods to each other.

Kensington was predominantly Jewish until after the Second World War when many of the more prosperous families moved north to Forest Hill. Postwar immigrants, mainly Ukrainians, Hungarians, Italians and Portuguese took their place in the market and gave the area a more international flavor.

In the early '60s there was another shift. Except for the Portuguese, most of the Europeans moved north and west. So, today the Kensington population consists mostly of Portuguese from the Azores, rapidly increasing numbers of Chinese displaced from the area of the New City Hall, a few blacks, and a scattering of Jews, Ukrainians, Hungarians and Italians.

The best time to visit Kensington is Friday afternoon or Saturday morning. The area is easily reached by public transit, or private automobile, but as a prelude to its spirit, why not treat yourself to a ride on the College streetcar. Toronto, by the way, is one of the last six cities in North America to operate a street-railway system, and boasts the largest fleet (358) of "P.C.C. Streamliners" in the world. P.C.C. of course, stands for Presidents Conference Car, as these streetcars were designed to the specifications of the heads of North American Public Transit Systems in the midthirties. Enjoy the rumble-screech sounds before they disappear and look at the car as an example of pre-war industrial design.

Get off at College and Spadina and pause to orient yourself.

Kensington lies south-west of College and Spadina, but before beginning your tour, consider a lunch at one of the local eateries. Our personal first choice is The Bagel where all the waitresses claim to be somebody's mother and fill you up with chicken

50

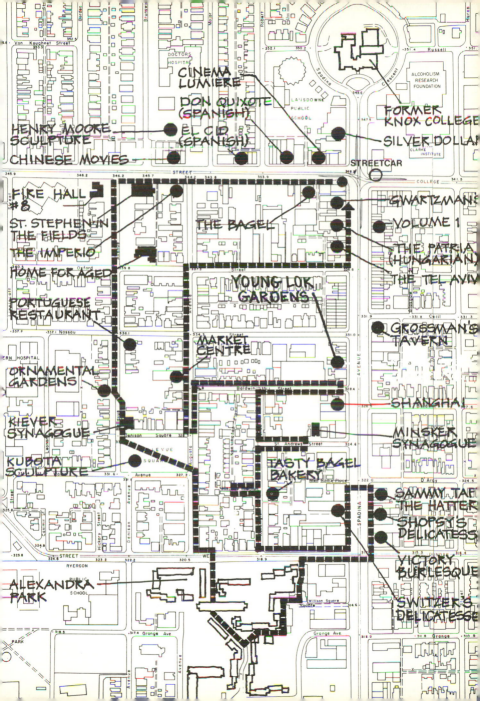

CINEMA LUMIERE

DON QUIXOTE (SPANISH)

EL CID (SPANISH)

HENRY MOORE SCULPTURE

CHINESE MOVIES

FORMER KNOX COLLEGE

SILVER DOLLAR

STREETCAR

FIRE HALL #8

ST. STEPHEN IN THE FIELDS

THE IMPERIO

HOME FOR AGED

PORTUGUESE RESTAURANT

ORNAMENTAL GARDENS

KIEVER SYNAGOGUE

KUBOTA SCULPTURE

THE BAGEL

YOUNG LOK GARDENS

MARKET CENTRE

GWARTZMAN'S

VOLUME 1

THE PATRIA (HUNGARIAN)

THE TEL AVIV

GROSSMAN'S TAVERN

SHANGHAI

MINSKER SYNAGOGUE

TASTY BAGEL BAKERY

SAMMY TAFT THE HATTER

SHOPSY'S DELICATESS

VICTORY BURLESQUE

SWITZER'S DELICATESSE

ALEXANDRA PARK

soup (on Fridays available with kreplach), kishka, fried fillet of white-fish, and blintzes with sour cream or applesauce. Other favorites include Shopsy's, Switzer's or the Tel-Aviv for delicatessen food, the Shanghai or Yung Luck for Chinese food and the El Cid for Spanish. If you enjoy wine with your meal, we suggest the Patria for Hungarian delights (served on weekends with 1930s Budapest-style music and dancing), the Don Quixote for Spanish and the Imperio for Portuguese.

The broad expanse of Spadina Avenue provides a strong north-south orientation to the area. The impressive width of the street is the result of the plan designed about 1815 by Dr. W.W. Baldwin, a physician who practised law and architecture on the side. He envisaged a tree-lined boulevard leading from the lake to Spadina House, his family estate, which stood near the site of Casa Loma. Politics being as they are, the trees never appeared, and Spadina never became the Champs Elysées.

Just north of College Street the buildings which originally housed Knox College, built in 1875, appear to be a well planned focal point for the head of Spadina; not so. The centre of the crescent was originally planned as a site for public ornamental gardens, but it was never developed and eventually was sold in 1873 for $10,000 to the Presbyterian Church. It was promptly filled with buildings.

The history of Spadina's past is very much evident on the face it presents today. Still surviving is the oldest Jewish book store in the city at number 412, and the shop of Sammy

Taft the world famous hatter at 303. The window of Gwartzman's Canvas and Art Supplies at 448 illustrates the changing nature of the area. This store formerly sold only dry goods, but now caters to the artists' community which has recently established itself in flats above the stores on Spadina. Chinese shops, displaced from Chinatown, are beginning now to appear along both sides of the street.

Two blocks west of College and Spadina is Bellevue, truly a fascinating street. At its head are the Philippine Sari-Sari Centre, St. Stephen-in-the-Fields Anglican Church (built ten years prior to Confederation and designed by the architect of the Ottawa Parliament Buildings) and the "Number 8" Hose Station which must be one of the most dramatic firehalls in the city. On Bellevue, on the north-east corner of Oxford, is a home for the aged, smack in the midst of the hustle and bustle. At Bellevue and Nassau Streets is a modest , but good Portuguese rest-aurant. On the west side of Bellevue, houses 48, 50 and 52 have front gardens containing lights, statuary and fountains which will be activated upon request.

At the foot of the street is Denison Square overlooked by the Kiever Synagogue built about 1914. In the south-west corner of the park is a steel sculpture by Nobuo Kubota, dedicated to Charlotte Hause who died a few

Top left: Bellevue Square; Top right; Kiever Synagogue; Bottom: Market produce at Kensington

Children playing in Kensington

years ago. She was closely associated with the community centre, St. Christopher House, and this sculpture was donated to the park by her friends.

To the south of Dundas Street is Alexandra Park which stands on an area declared a disaster zone in 1911, and which took over fifty years to be replaced by the City. Designed by our office in association with Klein and Sears, and Webb Zerafa Menkes, the project today provides subsidized rental housing for low income groups. By entering under the large apartment building near Dundas Street you can follow the paved pedestrian way through the project. Behind the row of houses is a large private park.

Now, head north on Kensington to the heart of the market area. Until the end of World War II there was shopping only on Kensington and Baldwin but it has subsequently spread into many of the surrounding streets. Be on the lookout for the Tasty Bagel Bakery opposite Fitzroy Terrace — a small lane leading off Kensington Avenue containing a few small but freshly painted row houses. Get an earful of Portuguese music and don't miss the Sansi Banana Company or the Yes Yes Yes Store. Other delights include the fish stores, Greek stores, Rumanian stores, Jamaican stores, chicken stores, bargain stores, junk stores, and rabbits on the streets with their fur hanging out.

There are fish, lobsters, clams, oysters, snails, smelts, pigeon eggs, raspberry syrup, herring, octopus, squid, live and dead plucked and unplucked chickens, corduroy pants, synthetic leather coats, oranges, lemons, apples, turnips, carrots, toma-

toes, pears, beets, smoked carp, white fish, salmon and pink fish with open mouths and staring eyes. Drop in for Portuguese records at 248 Augusta, or a banner of Jack and Bobby Kennedy in velvet at Lojamoderna. Purchase Swiss scenes, romantic gardens, nativity scenes, and tapestries with splashing nude ladies in rippling brooks, under the Kosher Meat and Poultry Store at 238 Augusta.

On St. Andrew Street there is an old Synagogue designed by Kaplan and Sprachman Architects. It is still in use and is one of the few remaining in the downtown area.

Looking west at the corner of Oxford and Augusta. On the north side is a brilliant lime green house. On the south side, a painted red facade, then a seafoam green facade, then a red, bright yellow, turquoise, a light yellow, a purple, red, dark pink and red brick.

For local entertainment try Chinese movies at the Electra, Rock and Roll at the El Mocombo or Country and Western at the Waverley. Ready for more? On the northeast corner of Dundas and Spadina, in a renovated building which once housed the Victory Burlesque Theatre, you can sample live Chinese theatre or shake your booty at the Lotus Lantern, Canada's first Chinese discotheque.

Further evidence of the rapidly growing Chinese community in this area ranges from street signs in oriental script to a bevy of Chinese restaurants. One of our favorites is Champion House, whose cooks come from all four regions of China. In addition to the best Peking duck in the city you should try the Mongolian hot pot, a sort of Chinese fondue, and a great way to beat the chills on a wintery day. You should also investigate the many Chinese shops in the area and be sure not to overlook the grocery stores and fish markets. Of further interest is the new Chinese Shopping Centre whose facades were imported from Hong Kong, located on the west side of Spadina south of Dundas.

To the east of the Chinese restaurant strip, along Dundas Street, is the new Art Gallery of Ontario. It houses the largest collection of Henry Moore works in the world, an art rental gallery, an excellent art book store and an attractive restaurant operated by the owners of the Three Small Rooms. If you are interested in the future of art you might step around the corner into the Ontario College of Art, located on McCaul Street, and brush denims with budding artists.

On the north side of Dundas, opposite the AGO, is a row of handsomely renovated Victorian houses that contain a number of private art galleries, the showroom of the Ontario Crafts Council and an interesting restaurant called Samina's Tiffen Room. This establishment offers Indian food in the English colonial style as it was cooked at the turn of the century.

If, at this point, you have tried everything we have suggested, your head is bursting with culture, you have sore feet and you have gained 10 pounds. Go home ... but come back another day.

St. Stephen-in-the-Fields Anglican Church

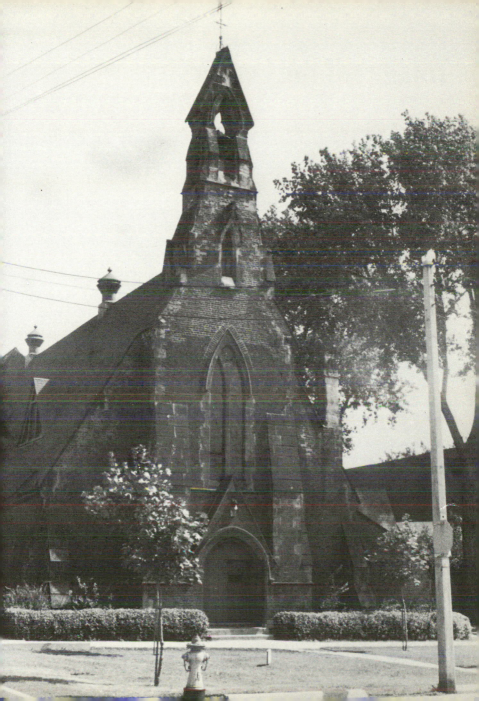

Images of the University

BY GEORGE BAIRD

How to "imagine" the University of Toronto? Hurried visitors on tour buses gather impressions of "picturesque" buildings set in green lawns. Habitués of nearby rooftop lounges at the Park Plaza and Sutton Place hotels read an urban forest penetrated by spires. New students often fail to sense any coherent image at all — particularly now that the huge, new John P. Robarts Research Library looms over the campus, calling into question almost all of the older building patterns which have made the University a distinctive midtown precinct.

One of the official images of the University is revealed by a map prepared by the Department of Information for campus visitors. This map is so everyday a part of getting to know the campus, and so poignant a piece of evidence of the University's effort to hold together a physical reality of which it has lost control, that I have used it as the base of the entrée to the campus I offer.

The University today covers a vast square-shaped territory stretching from Bloor Street on the north to College on the south, from Bay on the east to Spadina on the west. As the map implies, commercial parking around the periphery of the campus is reasonably convenient; parking with-

in the university precinct is not. The campus is served by both the Bloor and University Avenue subways, as well as the College Street streetcar, and the Spadina, Avenue Road, Bay and Wellesley buses.

Besides providing access to the University, these streetcar and bus routes offer an excellent means of getting a first sense of the shape of the campus. To travel around its perimeter start — say — at College and Spadina. Take the College streetcar east, along the Engineering/Science-/Medicine edge of the campus. Transfer to a Bay bus north and then again at Wellesley. The Wellesley bus route will take you to the heart of Queen's Park, past the Catholic and Methodist precincts of the University, then along Hoskin Avenue through the Anglican and back to the western edge of the new "west" campus. Now return to where you began via a Spadina bus south. It will take you down around the original base of University Presbyterianism, old Knox College, which still magisterially surveys lower Spadina Avenue.

At College and Spadina you might appropriately pause to eat in one of

Window over University College's main entrance

58

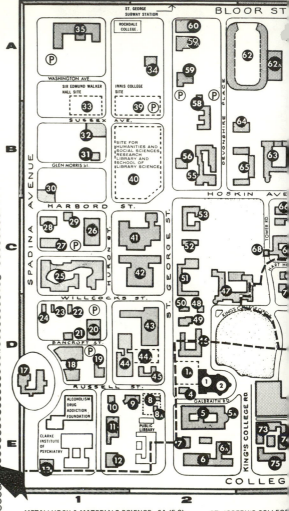

ALPHABETICAL LISTING

University of Toronto

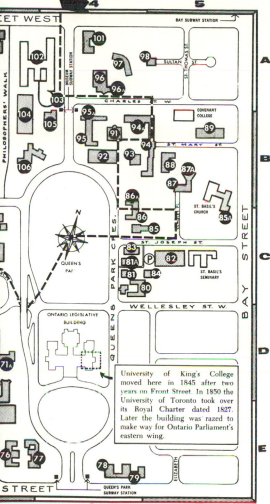

University of King's College moved here in 1845 after two years on Front Street. In 1850 the University of Toronto took over its Royal Charter dated 1827. Later the building was razed to make way for Ontario Parliament's eastern wing.

the varied, agreeable and inexpensive restaurants which surround the intersection.

During your meal, ponder the noticeably religious flavor of the campus. Although it is now rather faded and imprecise, religious differentiation is the oldest of all the University images. The University originated with King's College, which stood at the top of what is now University Avenue. In 1852, the Provincial Legislative Assembly voted to dissolve King's exclusive Church of England affiliation, to found, instead, an "absolutely secular institution" to be known as the University of Toronto. Shocked Anglicans responded by establishing their own "Trinity College." In 1856, Roman Catholics inaugurated St. Basil's Seminary and then, St. Michael's College; in 1875, Presbyterians erected the first Knox College building; and in 1881, Methodists moved their "Victoria University" from Cobourg to a new building at the top of the east side of Queen's Park. These original buildings, together with "University College" built to house the new "secular" university, and the School of Practical Science, determined the pattern of university building for the next half-century.

The early growth of the university was largely influenced by the grand residential neighborhood in which it was established. During the first half-century, all the colleges expanded around and into the great houses surrounding them. Even today, University College, Knox, Wycliffe, Vic-

Aerial view of campus grounds

toria and St. Michael's all embrace some of the houses among which they matured. Only in the second half-century of expansion has this practice been abandoned — unfortunately, for an ungracious, expedient policy of demolition and replacement.

Having established in your mind the square-shaped bounds of the university, now cut across the campus on the diagonal, from College and Spadina at the south-west to Avenue Road and Bloor at the north-east. Pass by the old Toronto Central Library at the corner of College and St. George.

Rounding the corner and proceeding up St. George Street, you will see, surrounded by the Faculty of Applied Arts and Engineering buildings, a mansion that was once the home of architect Frederick Cumberland. His masterpiece — University College — is the zenith of University of Toronto architecture, and of this tour.

Farther up the east side of St. George, open the heavy glass and metal doors of the new Knox College and cross through the arcade to the front vestibule. Here is one of the great university staircases, an architectural creation whose raison d'être is not fire safety or efficient circulation, but rather the celebration of entry and ascent. Now head for the solid front doors of Knox, and as you push them open watch, like Alice in Wonderland, the widening slot of light gradually reveal the full expanse of the view before you — the front campus.

This part of the campus is called "front" because it is the symbolic focus of the entire university, its "inside" outdoor space — the public centre of the "private" university precinct.

Strike out across it towards the tower of the old university library. Go up into the main reading room and stacks, or farther, up the main stairwell, to the second floor balcony. From here you may gaze out over the stairs to the front campus beyond. Back downstairs in the depths of the old stacks, if you peek out one of the intimate windows you can catch a glimpse of the vestigial gully of Taddle Creek. Taddle Creek used to wind through the campus from Bloor Street to College — it has long since been relegated to a sewer pipe.

Now for University College, the campus masterpiece — climb to the top of the UC main tower via the richest of all the university staircases. The first half of the ascent (to the level of the two great halls of the College) is public. To climb farther, obtain special permission from the College, and you will be shown a small staircase that will take you to the parapet.

Next, follow the echoing hallways of UC to the east doors, and out again to face the southern facade of Hart House. This was the Massey family's sumptuous and stylish gift to the male students of the university, and was one of the first structures to be built after the programmatic requirements of buildings and the conceptual capacities of the university's architects began to part ways.

Architecturally speaking, there are really three Hart Houses. To see Hart House as it was seen at the time of

---

Top: Arcade through Knox College
Bottom: Hart House

construction, explore its southern public wing. Pause particularly to sense the character of the Great Hall and the library — rooms of great sophistication yet disturbing in their self-conscious emulation of Oxbridge precedents. To see Hart House looking back to the great and unselfconscious tradition of University College and the old library, explore the northern athletic wing. The double level gymnasium is unmatched in formal sophistication anywhere in the world. Then explore the labyrinthine undercroft of the Hart House of the present. If you don't get lost in the passageways, you will discover a snack bar, a tuck shop, and even an entire theatre complex, socially active areas whose suppression is all too typical in character of most subsequent university buildings.

Extracting yourself from the architectural contradictions of Hart House, set out next across Queen's Park. If the front campus is the "public" outdoors of the university precinct, Queen's Park is the "public" outdoors of the whole midtown Toronto area. Here, students and teachers rub shoulders with Provincial government employees, Bloor Street shoppers, and Sutton Place socialites.

At the east side of the park are St. Michael's and St. Basil's, surrounding Elmsley Place, the most touching of all the relics of the former residential neighborhood. It comprises still almost an entire street, and serves as a domestic front gate to the whole St. Michael's precinct.

Back out on Queen's Park Crescent, follow the sidewalk straight on north (the street veers away to the left), and up the steps into the quadrangle of Victoria College. In the centre sits the original Victoria University building announcing through its ivy the profound 19th century Methodist conviction. "The truth shall make you free." Passing under this inscription, you find another great university staircase. This one is distinguished by the airy and easy generosity of the foyer to which it leads. Off this foyer are all the principal rooms of the original college.

Outside again, cross the Victoria quadrangle to the east, and follow the arcade of Burwash Hall out to Charles Street. This arcade, like the Knox one through which you have already passed, suggests a possible future pattern of gracious and convenient walkways for the whole university, a pattern which one can only hope will someday form a key part of the kind of building yet to come.

Consider ending your walking tour at the Roof Terrace of the Park Plaza hotel (Bloor and Avenue Road), where you will be able to relax with a drink in what, until it was recently "redecorated," was Toronto's most charming "thirties-moderne" decor. While you do, ponder the apocryphal tale which tells of the bankruptcy of the first of the two builders of the Park Plaza. He was unable to finance the repair of the foundations damaged by Taddle Creek which flows under the building before finding its subterranean way through the urban forest of the University beyond.

Yesteryear's architecture

The West Annex

BY JAMES ACLAND

In the mid-1800s, as Georgian squares and elegant row houses of Toronto's downtown began to give way to warehouses and shops, those who were making instant fortunes in trade and speculation began searching for a suburban idyll. Sherbourne and Jarvis were the first stops in the hasty retreat away from the sailors' stews of Queen Street and grog shops of the waterfront, but soon after the villages and open country beyond Bloor became ripe for speculation.

The village of Yorkville became an artisans' residential retreat, Rosedale was planned as a romantic garden suburb, and the Annex, a high-toned enclave for the new rich.

Albert Nordheimer, a piano merchant on King Street, was one of the first to come to the Annex. In the 1870s he built a house and coachhouse at the corner of Bloor and Avenue Road where once had stood an infamous Yorkville pub, the Tecumseh Wigwam. With a resident coachman and a fashionable conversion to the Anglican faith, he set the pattern for late Victorian Toronto: a large house with crockets, finials, tower and spires, set on a landscaped lot with a host of domestics, subdued children and bearded relatives seated in wicker garden chairs.

By 1890, Timothy Eaton, the up and coming dry good merchant, forsook the rather prosy and middle class purlieus of Orde and McCaul to build at 182 Lowther. He was joined by Joseph Patterson, an importer of men's furnishings. Shortly a host of men of property, bellies straining at the weskits, transformed the area into an Imperial preserve for the affluent gentry and their offspring. The names of the newcomers, Gooderham, Stollery, Hees, Baldwin, Burwash, Massey, Galbraith, Atkinson and Parkin amongst others still resound through the directorates and professions of today.

The successful merchants, land speculators and financial brokers who first came to the Annex looked to America for their architectural inspiration, away from the tired Victorian Gothic and debased Regency styles being built elsewhere by establishment "Compact" families.

These granitic Baptists and sturdy Presbyterians wanted strength and solidity: substance was all. Rock-faced masonry and elaborately carved sandstone, dark brick and russet-hued ashlar bulged and pressed over the entries to carry on intricate roofscape of arches, turrets, gargoyles, gables and gazebos. But, inside, the houses boasted high ceilings and suprisingly bright and cheerful interiors. Stripped

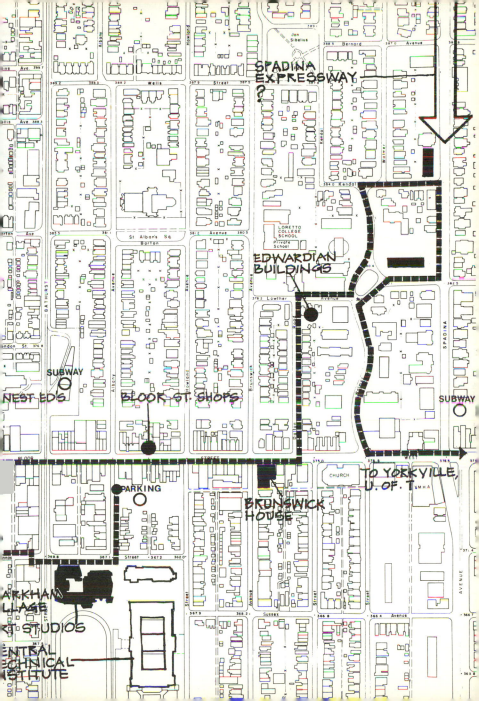

SPADINA
EXPRESSWAY
?

EDWARDIAN
BUILDINGS

SUBWAY

NEST EDS

BLOOR ST. SHOPS

SUBWAY

PARKING

TO YORKVILLE,
U. OF. T.

BRUNSWICK
HOUSE

ARKHAM
VILLAGE
STUDIOS

CENTRAL
TECHNICAL
INSTITUTE

of the clutter of "things" which made circulation a game and cleaning a major economic venture, the fine panelling and bright carving, the high windows and elegantly plastered ceilings had more than a suggestion of the new and exciting interlockings of space and material which were to emerge in Frank Lloyd Wright's prairie houses. They had hot and cold running water, bathrooms with flush toilets, roomy kitchens with immense ranges and capacious larders; and in attic and basement, in spare rooms and nooks and crannies they had SPACE to live and to hide and to breathe. Their descendants do not do so well.

The Edwardians (Edward VII came to the throne in 1901) emphasized private grandeur, but they had the wit to see that no good purpose was served by bringing every man's carriage downtown. Electric streetcar lines on Bathurst in 1894 and Spadina and Yonge in 1891 let the Annex build during the first decade of the 20th century in a dense and yet civil pattern which could accommodate the captain of commerce on Walmer or St. George, the professor on Admiral and the carpenter on Tranby. All used the trams. All supported public transport.

As late as 1923 a strong Annex Ratepayers Association could fight off a proposal to establish a hospital on Prince Arthur by fielding a team of the following names: Gooderham, Aird, Baker, Baldwin, Boswell, Brock, Cawthra, Jarvis, Laidlaw, Parkin and Wrong — but no Eatons: who had flown to higher ground as Sigmund Samuel, the scrap metal dealer, and a new generation of entrepreneurs moved in. Nordheimer's estate became the site of the Park Plaza Hotel and Chevys and Fords began to appear on the streets, tempting residents to dreams of country houses at Pickering and Hogs Hollow.

Between the wars, the bustling pride which had built the Annex, the Old City Hall and Queen's Park gave way to an era of timidity and small projects. Downtown became hopelessly clogged with warehouses and junky commercial properties. The new suburbs around Eglinton, the Beaches, and beyond sprawled over the horizon in a deadly, monotonous sea of builders' homes, fit for heroes from Passchendaele and Vimy.

However we may dislike the overwhelming pretensions of the Edwardians, no matter how repellent their stuffy religiosity, they did things on a grand scale. Not their fault that the survivors of the holocaust settled for tiny gains and small streets. As the large money left during the '20s, the Annex was left to clerks, tailors and tobacconists, a sprinkling of professors, widows of tycoons and Lester Pearson working away busily on the third floor of an Admiral Road walkup.

Top left: Posh Annex high-rise
Top right: Honest Ed's discount store
Bottom left: Walmer Rd. Baptist Church
Bottom right: Central Technical Institute

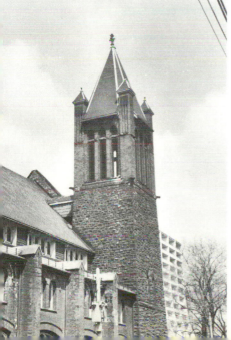

Bypassed by the automobiles which thunder up Avenue Road and St. George to exurban paradises, the Annex has maintained a precarious existence as an intown housing area. Adjacent to the expanding university, threatened by the commercial buildup along Bloor, a prime target for apartment developers because its old core is adjacent to the Bloor east-west subway, the Annex on either side of Spadina faces a major fight over the Spadina Expressway; a scheme which refuses to die.

One might well ponder upon the remarkably trivial role which the arts of design have played in the meteoric rise, fall and rebirth of this fashionable Toronto centre. In the end, the lack of parks, the lack of variety in street pattern, and the lack of a layout which could create protected cul-de-sacs condemned the area prematurely to loss of some of its major structures. And yet the Annex is being reborn as an attractive upper middleclass enclave, as rooming houses are converted to nifty town houses.

Remember that in most North American cities, 1890 fashionable streetcar suburbs have collapsed into wild anarchy and racially restricted slums where quite literally you walk in fear of your life. In Toronto, this area is an urban battleground between developers and residents, between highway engineers and urban ecologists, between theorists and pragmatists, but by a miracle, the streets remain safe. It is a cohesive, densely packed tangle of housing where communicators, educators, and a new breed of politicians meet night after night in a frantic blast of involvement.

IT'S GREAT . . . if a trifle exhausting.

To begin a tour of the west Annex, get to Lippincott south of Bloor (there's parking if you need it), then walk down to Lennox (named after the architect of the old 1890 City Hall). Drop into the art studios of Central Technical Institute by architects Robert Fairfield and Macy DuBois. Built in 1962, this building holds up well. The bold staggered studios and the masculine modelling made it a bellwether for the architecture of the '60s.

The Markham St. Village just around the corner is the creation of Ed Mirvish and his son David. The DM, David Mirvish Gallery, has an exciting large exhibit space and the exterior keeps the scale of the street. The whole complex of galleries, shops, restaurants, glass blowers and assorted nonsense is just right, even to the totem pole and the gas lamps. Splendid fun and games.

Next, Ed Mirvish's store at the corner of Markham and Bloor, Honest Ed's wacky world, is a magnificent refutation of the statement that there is no place for a skilled entrepreneur in the systematized 20th century. He's some man — he saved the Royal Alex theatre when the theatre buffs seemed willing to let it go down the drain. We are very much in his debt.

Bloor west, from Bathurst, is a rapid transit spine serving Greek, Italian and Portuguese territories. The line of the subway is marked by

Spired roofs

apartments — but hopefully the medium density terrace rows will be saved. When the east-west subway replaced the trams on Bloor, the street began to change from a scraggly strip to a surprisingly effective linear shopping mall. To the west along Bloor, there are stores, restaurants, markets, specialty shops and bookstores catering to the diverse multinational communities of the west side. They extend the rich hurly-burly of Kensington Market out to Dundas and beyond.

East along Bloor, from Bathurst to St. George, the pressure for a more intensive use of property brought by the rapid transit line has led to a linear strip of apartments and new shopping complexes. This is inevitable, but in the blocks of older Edwardian housing both north and south of Bloor, there is a splendid series of dense, low-rise villages of row housing and new habitats, amidst the predominantly high-rise strips. The gritty texture of sandstone, pyramidal roofs, turrets and a fascinating variety of architectural details make these older houses, churches and halls a visual asset in a city which is becoming increasingly dominated by anonymous walls of glass and concrete towering into the sky. Socially more important, these old houses can flex, adapt and change over the years.

Designed for large families, they are cut first to separate apartments and then to roomers. Surprisingly, many are now reverting to single family occupancy, suggesting an enhanced and new life for older areas in the city.

The big estates have proven the most difficult to save. Along Walmer and Lowther, close to the Spadina subway entrance, many of the Edwardian mansions have been replaced by one well-known Toronto architect's own variant of Super-Pop apartments. His answer to the fearsome sameness of developers' apartments was to tack cut-out metal screens on balconies. Tiring of this he turned to rococo curves on projecting shear walls. I suppose all this is relatively harmless, even if phenomenally ugly. But it's sad to see architectural talent wasted on paper-thin superficial decoration in lobbies and balconies which leave the basic highrise block untouched. The real problem is to create new and more humane high density housing in the city by a total reconsideration of plan and structure.

Local residents have banded together to catalogue all housing in the Annex as a basis for a citizen planning study. They are determined to keep the Annex a viable part of the urban fabric. They do not want it to become another St. James Town development. All their efforts will prove fruitless if the Spadina Expressway — the famous route from nowhere to nowhere — is ever rammed through. The Annex, Kensington, Spadina and all this area will be drowned in a flood of autos pouring off the expressway and the local residents have fought back with some energy. If we can't save the Annex we might as well kiss our cities goodbye . . . and all move up to Frobisher Inlet.

No. 4 Prince Arthur

The Village of Yorkville

BY JACK DIAMOND

Yorkville, as you might guess from its name, was once a village. Its centre stood where Yorkville Avenue and Yonge Street now meet. Originally it was where a toll gate for those travelling along long, straight Yonge Street, carved out in 1793 to connect the town of York — as Toronto was then known — with Lake Simcoe. Only two civic buildings still exist from those early days — the fire hall and library.

Unlike much of Toronto, history has not played an important part in the development of this area, for although the older buildings provide the framework for what is there, present functions are almost completely new. Yorkville is entirely a creature of today, and it is its continual "recycling" process that makes the area as fascinating as it is.

Before taking a closer look at the phenomenon of Yorkville, it is interesting to examine what it is about Toronto that has allowed an area like Yorkville to exist. Toronto, unlike most other North American cities, or European ones for that matter, does not have a single centre with its apex of activities declining in regular waves to the suburbs. Any map will illustrate that Toronto is multi-centered; but in spite of this, there are those who insist on seeing it in a bicycle-wheel form.

And because radial-patterned cities seem to require throughways driven into their hearts to make automobile commuting easy, monumental expressways and complex cloverleaves have become the status symbols of quaint municipal politicians — and the destruction wrought in the path of this "progress" has been accepted as a necessary casualty.

Fortunately there are some who have opposed outmoded forms of progress and Toronto has, at times, been saved from the insensitive centrifuge which would fling out the healthy, constituent parts of the city compound into separate isolated parts, into clinically pure elements. What we have is messy and human, not clean and brutal. Such an area so saved is Yorkville and the Annex adjacent.

The characteristics of this healthy city are there for all to see: a collection of districts with centres of character and interest. Each has the spectrum of facilities needed by residents. Each caters to the transient day-time population. And many have developed a speciality which caters to a regional market. Thus there is no need for us all

A pleasant diversion for York Square's shoppers

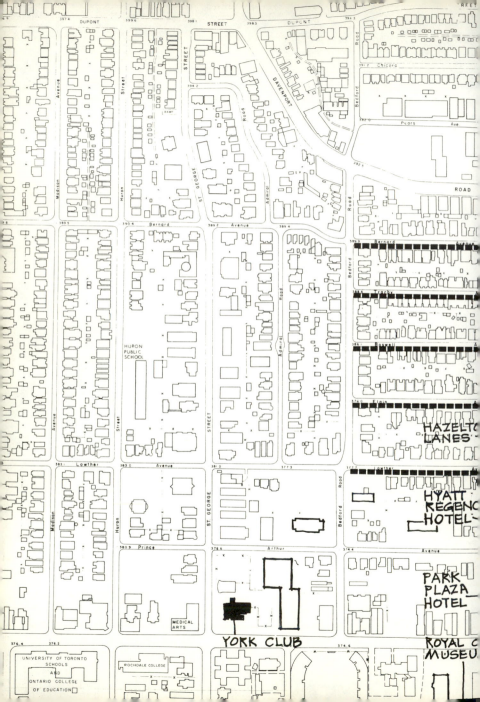

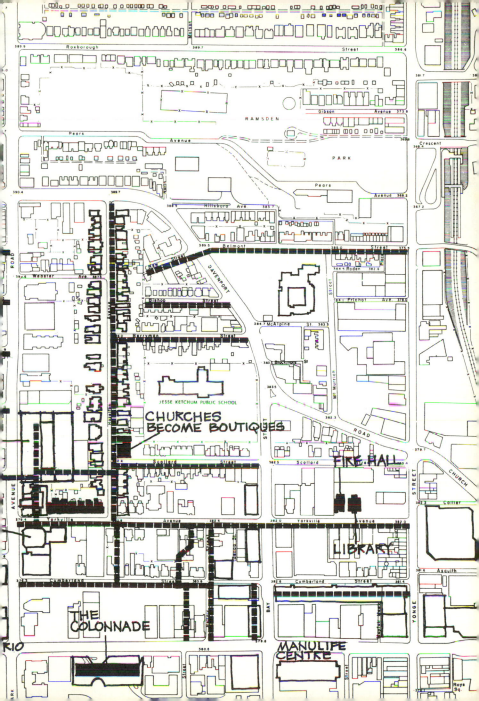

CHURCHES
BECOME BOUTIQUES

JESSE KETCHUM PUBLIC SCHOOL

FIRE HALL

LIBRARY

THE
COLONNADE

RIO

MANULIFE
CENTRE

to get to one place at one time.

A further benefit accrues to our multi-centred pattern because each of Toronto's centres is no more than that required for the accommodation of its speciality and local needs. Thus, these centres co-exist with much smaller, nearby low-density housing and small scale commercial buildings. The genius of Toronto is indeed to have these pockets about 1½ miles apart on major arterial routes, with housing distributed throughout the regions between. The streets that service these small scale areas are commensurably small, appropriately intimate, sympathetically human in concern, rather than efficient in technological outlook.

The Bloor/Yonge/Yorkville area exhibits all these characteristics like a casebook. All ingredients are there, interacting with superb effect. Bloor Street, of large scale, is the location for haute couture, and other expensive, elegant stores. It is served by the subway. Nearby are the boutiques and art galleries accommodated in Victorian houses on Yorkville Avenue and Cumberland Street, or in intrablock walkways. And behind them the narrow streets like Bishop, Scollard, Berryman, Tranby, Bernard, Hazelton and Lowther ("progress" should be equated, in this context, with narrowing streets, rather than widening them), lined by trees and old rehabilitated two – or three-storey houses.

Some of the renewal in the area is sensitive, some not. For instance,

Nucleus of old Yorkville

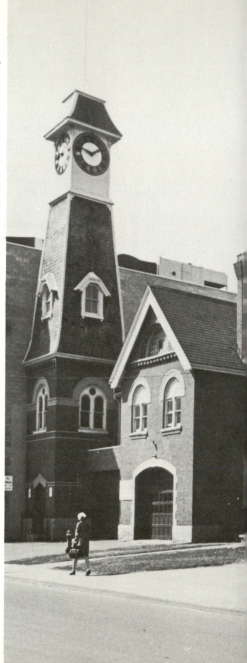

Typical residential street

houses that lie west of Hazelton on Yorkville Avenue have been crudely clad in "designers" knobly brick. This is, perhaps, an acceptable compromise if the alternative were destruction, which originally was the intent of this developer. The houses had become decayed, through deliberate or unconscious neglect, and a Pied Piper strategy was presented to the city fathers — a bag of gold (higher zoning) for ridding the city of rat-infested houses. Fortunately, by that time it had been demonstrated nearby that low density development was feasible and the city was, for once, saved from being saved.

However, the thing that attracts development is sometimes the very thing that is destroyed by the development: the charm and human scale, the variety of uses of appeal to a wide range of income groups that characte-

rised Yorkville is in danger of eclipse — new development is too large or too dense, and the retail uses, now taking over almost all space in the area, are exclusively for the carriage trade.

The way many of the activities still co-exist, however, is exemplary. Houses, shops, art galleries, restaurants live side by side as do shops, restaurants, theatres, offices and apartments stacked above each other, as in the Colonnade with its second-storey mall. The mixed uses do not conform to neat city planning maps with orderly, distinct blobs of color, each representing a separate land use. They do conform, however, to life and its complexities.

It would be a mistake to carefully describe a route to be followed in the Yonge Street-Yorkville area. Much of its delight lies in surprise, and discovery. The map suggests streets to visit

York Club

rather than individual buildings to watch for, for as you will discover when you wander along, it's not so much the architectural gems that give this area its flavor, but the harmonious way collections of buildings and streets co-exist.

Careful observation, however, will reveal some fascinating details — Victorian gingerbread, modern pop, good modern things and schocky modern things, authenticity and kitsch. Perhaps of greatest value is to see how small places, narrow streets and indirect passageways work, how the intricacy of the networks succeed where the obvious, conventional shopping plaza and stereotype apartment would fail.

Art Galleries

1. Carmen Lamanna *840 Yonge Street*
2. Electric *272 Avenue Road*
3. Isaacs *832 Yonge Street*
4. Moos *138 Yorkville Ave*
5. Morris *15 Prince Arthur*
6. Innuit *30 Avenue Road*
7. Laing *194 Bloor West*
8. Mitchell *27 Prince Arthur*
9. Roberts *641 Yonge Street*
10. Albert White *25 Prince Arthur*
11. Atelier *110 Cumberland*
12. Frederick Thom *194 Bloor West*
13. Galerie Dresdnere *130 Bloor West*
14. Gallery Pascal *104 Yorkville*
15. Lilliam Morrison *104 Cumberland*
16. Penell *13 Hazelton Ave*
17. Nancy Poole *16 Hazelton Ave*
18. Marlborough
    Goddard *13 Hazelton Ave*

The Nature Trails of Rosedale

BY EBERHARD ZEIDLER

Wild roses covered the hillsides around the home of Colonel William Botsford Jarvis. His wife was so enchanted with the beauty she decided to name her house Rosedale.

That was in 1874. The Jarvis estate extended from Yonge Street to Lamport Avenue and from Roxborough Street to Park Road. Now 100 years later you will look in vain for the wild roses. But, although they have long since disappeared, the ravines have survived and through the years have formed a natural protection for the unique charm of the Rosedale area. They have helped to save it from destruction in the middle of a growing metropolis. Its winding streets and beautiful trees are still there for you to enjoy and the houses speak of a period of Canadian affluence that had not yet found its own tradition and was searching for its roots in British history.

Prior to 1850 there was only one house in South Rosedale but by 1875 there were 10 and at the end of the century another 70 had been built. In 1909, the construction of a bridge over the Park Drive ravine opened North Rosedale, and in 1912 Moore Park was annexed to the city. Prior to, and after World War I, Rosedale mansions increased in number and a great many of Toronto's well-to-do moved in. There are now parks where mansions used to stand to remind us of an era past. Craigleigh Gardens, a 13-acre estate, was the home of the eminent family of lawyers, the Oslers, until 1924. Chorley Park, a 57-room mansion constructed in 1915, was the official residence of the Lieutenant Governor until 1937.

Rosedale not only attracted the wealthy — a number of modest houses, some quite ingeniously planned with rear access to lots and communal parking areas, were constructed around the same time.

The first expansion boom after the Second World War pushed people into suburbs and seemed to leave Rosedale to a Sleeping Beauty existence. Yet instead of roses, taxes grew and a changing economy made it difficult to maintain the old homes. One by one, many larger homes changed into rooming houses. The old glory tarnished and it appeared that the winding ways of Rosedale would follow the fate of many other stately streets in Toronto. Instead, yet a different pattern developed.

Young families, tired of suburban houses and the distance from downtown, in search of proximity and extra

Some of the beauties of the ravine

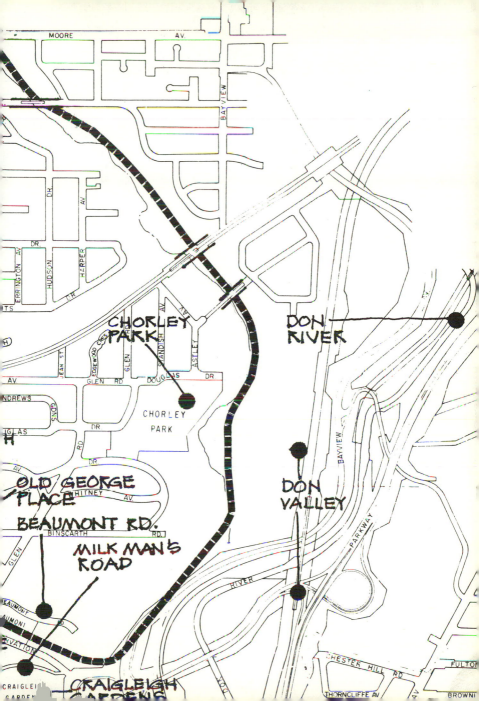

MOORE AV.

BAYVIEW

CHORLEY PARK

DON RIVER

CHORLEY PARK

DON VALLEY

OLD GEORGE PLACE

BEAUMONT RD.

MILK MAN'S ROAD

BAYVIEW

PARKWAY

RIVER

HESTER HILL RD.

FULTON

THORNCLIFFE AV.

BROWNI

CRAIGLEIGH GARDENS

bedrooms, rediscoverd Rosedale's rambling homes and nearly overnight its streets were filled again with children. No one group claimed Rosedale as its domain, thus creating an atmosphere of individuality with each house reflecting its own personality. But who can forecast the future — pressures and increasing land values may disturb this balance, which would be regrettable.

It is more by accident than by foresight that the ravines have been saved but they are wonderful in allowing us to escape from the bustling midtown traffic into the peace of meandering country-like valleys. The ravines are one of Toronto's greatest assets. We must treasure these incongruities that nature has given us and preserve their beauty for the enjoyment of all.

The ravine walk described here is, at present, only a "U" within more than 200 acres of parkland. Most of the major entrances into the park can be reached by subway and streetcar. As the ravines have only been developed in parts, some pioneering spirit is necessary to find your way through these enchanted valleys. Yet, if you explore with imagination, you will be rewarded. You may even forget you are in the middle of an urban area. There are vistas through trees — imposing arches of bridges — running brooklets and wild life. I have often found here Canadian wood ducks in the middle of winter. Only occasionally does an apartment tower appear like a distant castle above the trees to remind you that you have not totally escaped. Sunrise and sunset will throw long shadows across the valley. In winter, you will explore silently a fairyland — in spring, wild flowers abound on the south side with the remnants of snow remaining on the north. Summer will silently engulf the valley in its lush growth and finally the vibrant color burst of autumn.

The map indicates some of the key entrances accessible by public transportation — but there are numerous other points from which you can begin or end your walk. A three mile walk should take no longer than two hours.

From Heath Street — get to it from Yonge — at its east dead end you will find winding steps leading into the ravine bottom. From there you will pass the nature playground of Deer Park School, with the arches of the St. Clair bridge visible in the distance. The path will climb and meet with the St. Clair and Avoca Avenue entrance. Going south you enter Balfour Park which will take you below the Summerhill Railroad Bridge. At this point you cross Mount Pleasant Road and enter Park Drive ravine. A few years ago magnificent willow trees created an enchanting walk along the water but, unfortunately, "engineering improvements" to the brook have killed most of these. Yet, still remaining is the quiet charm of the ravine itself. To your north you will see between the trees a number of interesting houses — new and old — which you might want to explore in more detail. Streets such as Roxborough Drive, Old George Place and Beaumont Road are all worthy of sidetrips. Returning to the ravine you will pass under the vaulting

The ravine provides a pleasant and quiet retreat

arch of Glen Road Bridge. At the end of Park Drive you may wish to take the Milk Man's Road to the south, and walk back into Craigleigh Gardens and take a bus back to St. Clair and Yonge.

If, however, you wish to continue, you now enter the Don Valley. You will skirt along the edge of one of the Don Valley Parkway ramps and for a short while will have to your east the feeder roads to the expressway and the old brick works; to your west the treed slopes of the valley. You can, at some point along this path, turn north into another ravine leading up to Chorley Park. The Rosedale-Summerhill bus, which connects with the Yonge Street subway line, stops at the corner of this park. If you don't exit at Chorley Park, and wish to continue along the path you will by now have passed the Don Valley Brick Works and again be enclosed in a narrow ravine. Below Governor's Bridge and the Summerhill Railroad Bridge you will continue back up through the park until you reach Moore Avenue and the end of your walk.

One day I hope you will be able to continue this walk through the Mount Pleasant Cemetery back in a loop to your starting point at Heath Street and Deer Park School. This ravine walk would then connect with some of the other ravines that interlace Toronto.

There are also many interesting walks through South Rosedale, each one a discovery through winding streets.

Many things contribute to the fascinating character of Rosedale. Most important and probably unique for a North American city is its immediacy to downtown; in fact, Bloor Street, the major midtown centre, accepts its presence with a bow. Like the moats of a castle, the ravines define clearly the territory of Rosedale. Yet, the complexity and maybe oddity of its houses is the true charm of this district. I am sure that anyone unfamiliar with Canadian architecture will be shocked by his first aquaintance with it. All rules seem to have been turned upside down, yet it grows on you and in time you will see its uniqueness. No period was ever accepted but all are there: the Georgian, the Victorian fantasy, the Tudor and all else. At times it looks like a happy sample catalogue of architectural styles. You may want to see Chestnut Park where more than half a century ago hydro wires were put below grade and quaint street lamp fixtures were added to create charm. Here was also the beginning of St. Andrew's College. Where Avondale and Rosedale Roads meet you will find the interesting old gate house of the Jarvis Estate. The eastern part of Collier Street just outside Rosedale is an example of how the actions of a neighborhood and architects have saved a charming street. Ancroft Place at the junction of Sherbourne Street and the Rosedale ravine is an excellent example of how density can be achieved without destroying the neighborhood — unfortunately the townhouse schemes of today seldom reach the scale of perfection this small group has achieved.

55 Glen Road

Don Vale

BY IRVING GROSSMAN

My childhood image of the area now called Don Vale was of a place to stay away from. It was part of the "east end," which this skinny boy saw as a tough, hostile world. To venture east of Yonge Street was pretty bold, but to go east of Parliament was certain to mean trouble — a bloody nose, or at the very least, a scary chase back to the familiar streets of the Jewish districts. In any case, there certainly could be no promise of delicatessens where kids could nurse soft drinks, and play the pinball machine while enjoying — for free — aromas of chicken soup and steamed corned beef. So why go?

Oddly enough, while threats of bloody noses have all but disappeared, the same question might well be asked by anyone today looking for an interesting walking tour. For Don Vale offers little of the glamour of other downtown areas. It is a very old working class residential section dating back before the 1850s. Much of it is prosaic, cluttered, even seedy. Until recently, even its most charming buildings were disguised by the effects of neglect and hardship, and none have been considered worthy of the select list of the Toronto Historical Board. So why go?

The answer for me lies both in Don Vale's very modesty and in its story of survival. The narrow streets and cul-de-sacs, the small scaled houses, the peculiar — at times bizarre — variety of forms and detail, the clutter itself, possess a certain honest, human, unpretentious feeling, that one rarely finds in more elaborate settings. And in its survival; Don Vale has experienced a process which has meshed together a variety of life styles with one thing in common — a real commitment to downtown life.

If you look at the city map, you'll see that Don Vale is actually a well-defined pocket, bounded by the open green spaces of St. James' Cemetery to the north, the Don Valley to the east, the apartment neighborhoods of Regent Park to the south and St. James Town to the west. Unlike these neighbors, however, this area has survived the intense pressures for development. In the 1960s, when the City pronounced it an "urban renewal area", local residents and aldermen reacted and caused delays and enough uncertainties to discourage developers from moving in. Buyers in search of modestly priced downtown houses meanwhile were being attracted to the area. Unpretentious houses, sometimes in dreadful condition, could be acquired relatively cheaply, so refurbishing began. By the time the City lifted renewal designation, land was too expensive for developer assembly

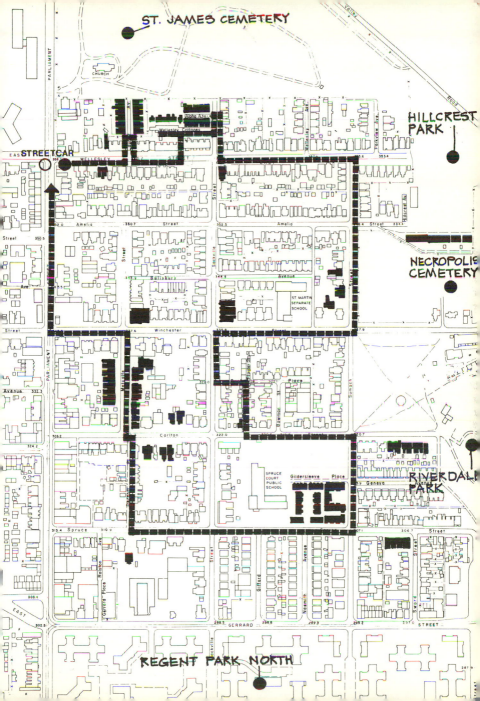

ST. JAMES CEMETERY

HILLCREST PARK

NECROPOLIS CEMETERY

RIVERDALE PARK

REGENT PARK NORTH

STREETCAR

CHURCH

PARLIAMENT

Alpha Ave.
Wellesley Cottages

WELLESLEY STREET

Amelia Street

Amelia Street

Salisbury Avenue

ST MARTIN SEPARATE SCHOOL

Winchester Street

Carlton Place

Bowman St.

Carlton

Spruce Street

SPRUCE COURT PUBLIC SCHOOL

Gildersleeve Place

Geneva Avenue

Gerrard Place

Rolston Place

Gifford Street

Nasmith Avenue

GERRARD

Sackville Street

Sumach Street

and opinion solidly unified against such a process. Don Vale was saved, even though some original residents were displaced by the incoming "white painters." And the young professionals and businessman attracted to the area brought a new spirit of optimism about its future.

Historically, Don Vale was part of the large park reserve established when the town of York was first built (1790). It was by-passed by the early growth of Yonge Street and although subdivided in the 1830s, it had only some 75 dwellings by 1858. Fifteen acres for the Necropolis was sold by the City in 1855, to a private concern for $16,000. In 1864, the tradition of local citizen action started as Don Vale residents objected so strenuously to the City selling more parkland to the cemetery that they forced the buying back of the property, creating what is now part of Riverdale Zoo.

A Boulton Atlas of the mid-1800s clearly reveals the intentions of early subdividers. It shows their own homes located on the corners of their estates in anticipation of further land divisions. Indeed, during Toronto's boom of the late '80s, the area filled up and, before the turn of the century many of the frame dwellings were replaced by handsome brick ones — a familiar story.

Most houses built after 1875 remain today, and are evidence of what we would now call "infill" housing, where backyards of estates were built up with cottages and tall rowhouses, at varying densities. This accounts for the present day diversity of house styles and sizes in close proximity — a kind of mixed bag of goodies, at times fun, but which also reaches the limits of incongruity.

Small wonder the area does not make the Historical Board list.

To get a feeling for the area I suggest a walk which will take between one and two hours. If you are driving, park your car on Wellesley, just east of Parliament; public transport can also get you to this corner. If you want something to nibble on while walking, stock up at the corner tobacconist. Start by walking east — you'll soon pass 321-323 Wellesley, tiny one-storey brick cottages with peaked roofs (also found in other parts of the city at times in stucco) built about 1885. Facing these on the north side is 314 Wellesley, an interesting three-storey brick house with weird grotesqueries of brick carving over the entry and around the upper windows.

The first cross street you meet is Laurier, a typical narrow cul-de-sac that has been fully refurbished by various owners. Some of these homes — now quite expensive — were not so long ago purchased for as little as $10,000, and sold (without any improvements being made) for as much as $25,000 three years later.

Further east, stroll up the little Wellesley Cottages street, reminiscent of an English village, to find a row of charming one-storey homes built about 1888. Apparently these were originally owned by one person and rented out as low income housing. To

Doorways you'll encounter on your tour

One of Don Vale's early homes

find such cottages still standing in a major city is remarkable. May they live long!

Nearby is Alpha Avenue, another cul-de-sac, this time of identical two-storey houses built also about 1888. The narrowness of the street, the upper storeys of slate shingles, the proportions of windows, the fenced rear courts, all create a charm and intimacy not to be found in most new housing projects. Remove the parked cars, and I think this street would be almost ideal.

Further east, past another cul-de-sac, Wellesley Avenue, you pass a range of houses: the ordinary, the charming, the peculiar, with all various tastes of past and present occupants on display. The east end of Wellesley Street is a good place to picnic. The park with wading pool and playground offers a panoramic view of the Don Valley, and although you now see the polluted Don River dominated by a noisy six-lane expressway, you can at least reminisce about the surveyors, who laid out these streets, fishing there for salmon.

Turning south on Sumach, past more "Alpha"-type houses mixed in with larger homes, you will reach Amelia Street which on your left leads to Hillcrest Park. Here, where once stood a glue factory, is a row of houses, all renovated and sold by one spec-builder. Front doors face the park rather than a roadway, which is really a worthwhile planning idea.

Along the west side of Sumach, facing the Necropolis and well set back from the roadway, is a row of taller homes, all under renovation, with richly varied facades and colours.

Typical Metcalfe house

Turning west onto Winchester, you pass one of the typical larger homes of 1880. At the corner of Sackville stands an unusual three-storey apartment of '30s vintage, with heavy brown balconies. One hears rumor that you can see traces of an older building incorporated in the detailing. I've looked carefully but can't find any.

Down Sackville, and detouring through lanes and Woodstock Place, you will reach a jewel of a two-storey house at 314 Carlton, built about 1875. Its proportions and details are quite beautiful. At Sumach again,

facing the old zoo entrance, is a row of houses that exhibit the energy of the various new owners. The early vitality of these tall buildings has been restored by sandblasting and painting.

At Spruce and Sumach, you will meet one of Toronto's first low-cost housing projects designed by the prolific housing architect Eden Smith and built about 1913 by private philanthropists. The gentle scale of these buildings, the porches, the courts and privacy are all worthwhile qualities.

Looking east along the south side of

Spruce, you see another row of "Alpha"-type houses (nos. 119-133). This time, heavy "eyebrows" over the ground floor windows add a touch of gaiety.

A glance down Nasmith and Gifford Street, both built up in the typical 1920s style, reveals houses with heavy porches and round columns — comfortable but undistinguished. In this area was the original Toronto General Hospital, torn down and relocated about 1910. In the distance, beyond Gerrard Street, can be seen the low apartment buildings of the early Regent Park public housing project. At 35 Spruce, sitting quietly on the remains of its estate behind a hedge and an elegant wrought iron railing and gate, you'll discover a most charming old farmhouse. Built about 1870, this one-and-one-half storey dwelling has beautifully proportioned windows and entrance doors, brick quoins on the corners. For me, it reveals a lot of the early atmosphere of this area. Facing this house is a narrow lane called Dermott Place in which you find a few more cottages and another early stucco farmhouse. At Carlton, a short detour to the east will take you past some good examples of the early grand houses dating from 1868-75.

Metcalfe is one of the most attractive of all the streets of this period with its arched trees closing over the roadway. The east side consists of three-storeyed gabled brick dwellings, well restored with window arches, and details intact; scrollwork and stained glass windows; sandblasted brick; and stained wood fences. The west side is now beginning its rebirth.

Set back from the street just below Winchester, hemmed in by its neighbors, sits a huge house showing a confusion of classical pediments, ionic columns, porches and much glass. Sadly in need of repair, it's a shabby shell of past splendor and pretention. I hope it soon will find some new owner to lavish it with attention.

At Winchester, is the large Donvale Community Centre Building, which was converted a few years ago from a little-used church. This massive dark brick edifice, of pre-1900 vintage, with its many arched windows and huge bell tower, now vibrates with community activities — a theatre, co-op nursery, crafts studio, co-op supermarket, etc. It also witnesses the meetings of the Don Vale Ratepayers group, an active and outspoken organization representing a cross section of the area's population.

Back on Parliament Street, you'll see on the west side a row of three-storeyed houses, with mansard roofs and beautiful decorative ironwork along the skyline — gutsy details, handsome proportions, but not yet displaying signs of refurbishing. Hope they survive.

Your tour can be rounded off by dropping into the nearby old Winchester Hotel, where the spirit of the old Don Vale is still very much in action. But be careful, the action can be a little rough if you stay too late. A stroll up Parliament past interesting "earthy" shops will take you back to your starting point.

Nobility of Parliament Street

Don Mills
An Experiment in Living

BY JOHN C. PARKIN
ASSISTED BY SYLVIA SKELDON

At the end of World War II, the sale of a large tract of land at the corner of Don Mills Road and Lawrence Avenue to Canadian Breweries signalled the start of a new epoch of land development in the Don River valley previously inhabited by farmers and mill operators.

The company originally intended to use its property for a brewery but the persuasive chairman E.P. Taylor urged that more land be purchased and a community be developed instead. In this way Don Mills — formerly known as Yorktown — was born. Don Mills was an experiment in living. Its aim was to make possible the healthy and happy coexistence of man, nature and machine.

It was a pioneer concept in many ways, incorporating several revolutionary ideas which, although now accepted as standard practice, caused a considerable stir in the Council Chambers when first presented. Pollution control was of major concern — at a time when ecology was a word known only to the initiated few. The North York Council was asked to approve strict control governing noise levels, outside storage, unsightly signs, provision of ample parking spaces, types of building materials and standards of architectural design. Finally, due in no small measure to the efforts

of Reeve McMahon, the Council agreed to the project and in 1954 the Don Mills Development company began the first planned community in Canada. Since then, this community has won many awards.

Whether the original aims of the Don Mills experiment have been realized is very much a subjective decision — and one deserving serious consideration during your tour of the area.

The very nature of the area means that any comprehensive tour must be split into two stages: both can be taken in one day, but I personally do not recommend such an energetic venture unless you plan to include liberal self-administrations of first aid in one of the comfortable lounges at the Inn on the Park. Regardless of your reasons for being there, the Inn makes an excellent starting and finishing point.

For the first stage of the tour, you will need either a bicycle or a comfortable pair of walking shoes ... although both would be ideal. You are going to explore the parks and residential areas bordering the western branch of the Don. Before entering Wilket Creek Park at the gateway opposite the Inn, pause for a while at the junction of Leslie and Eglinton and look around you. Remember the buildings, road systems,

100

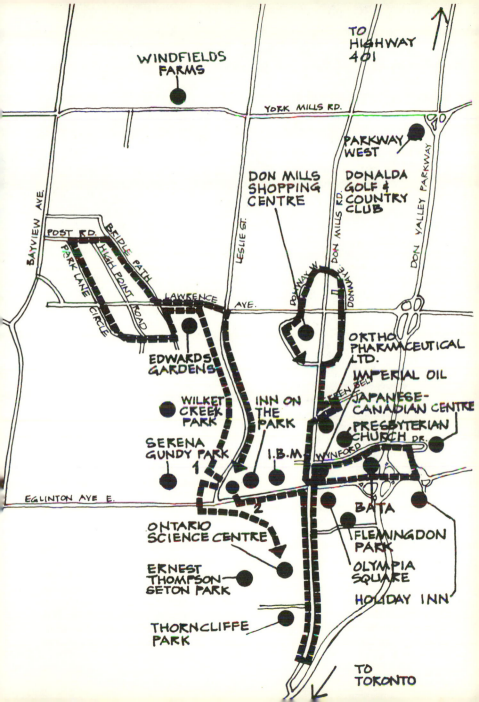

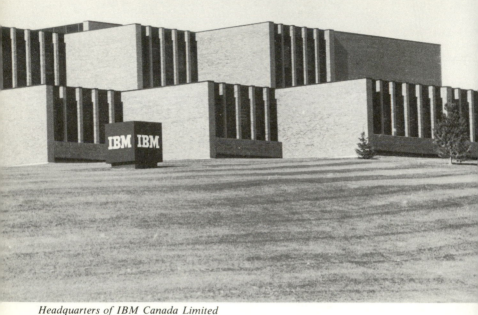

Headquarters of IBM Canada Limited

years, whichever comes first.

Return to the Inn on the Park by either retracing your steps through the parks or walking south along Leslie Street. There are some worthwhile office buildings on the east side of Leslie, notable among them being the Wrigley Building, designed by Gordon Adamson.

There is one more excursion worth the effort, perhaps negotiable after your brief stop at the Inn. Enter Wilket Creek Park again, this time turning left under Eglinton Avenue. This will bring you into Ernest Thompson Seton Park and a magnificent view of the Ontario Science Centre.

Now for the second phase of this tour — you should either bicycle or drive.

The major part of Don Mills and Flemingdon Park is best viewed by car since these two communities were also the pioneer attempts by Metropolitan Toronto to rationalize the use of the car, both through the total use of the cul-de-sac system — a hierarchy of roads based upon traffic needs — and the provision of parking — in many instances on well landscaped lots.

Start your road tour from the Inn on the Park, designed in its various stages by Webb Zerafa Menkes Housden, and drive east along Eglinton. On the left is a series of buildings by the Parkin firms. These, in sequence, are the headquarters of IBM Canada Limited, the regional headquarters of Imperial Oil Limited and

A dunk in the Don

the international headquarters of Bata, the world's largest shoe company.

At the south-west corner of Don Mills and Eglinton, with ample parking available, is the Ontario Science Centre, designed by Raymond Moriyama — an outstanding example of reinforced concrete in various textures and forms. The Science Centre is one of the most significant in the world. A day can be spent here in appreciation of the extraordinary impact of science on every-day life.

Across the road from its entrance are the twin towers of Olympia Square, designed by Bregman & Hamann, Architects, and to the south, Irving Grossman's pioneer, and deservedly well-recognized housing complex, Flemingdon Park. (see Chapter 10)

At the south end of Don Mills Road, before it descends into the valley to join the Don Valley Parkway, there are interesting new examples of systems building. On the left is the start of a large complex of housing, using some of the most advanced techniques of systems design; whereas, to the immediate right, is a public school of precast concrete assemblies, perhaps more noteworthy for its technology and innovation than design refinement.

Returning north along Don Mills Road, past Eglinton, the first major intersection is Wynford Drive. Exploration of the area reveals a vast assembly of building types: medical communication systems; then take the path that leads to the cool greenness of the valley floor. The contrast in visual and audio stimulation is almost overwhelming.

Explore the paths at your own pace, moving northward until you leave the natural woodlands of Wilket Creek for the groomed lawns and banks of many-hued flowers of Edwards Gardens. If you are on a bicycle, you must dismount for this last stretch of parkland ... but it is really no hardship.

The Gardens used to be the site of a three-storey mill built by Alexander Milne in 1817. The volume of water in the creek proved insufficient, however, and Milne later abandoned this site for one on the main branch of the river. Unfortunately, nothing now remains of the original building.

Rupert Edwards purchased the site of Milne's first mill in 1944. He erected a 500-foot rockery and built two dams to provide adequate water supply points around the grounds through the use of a large steel water wheel. In 1955 he sold the 27-acre site to Metropolitan Toronto for use as a park, and it was opened to the public in 1956. Some of the original buildings from the Rupert Edwards Estate are still standing although the residence, formerly used by the Garden Club of Toronto for the Civic Garden Centre, was burned down in 1962. As part of a Winter Works Incentive Program for 1963-64, authorization was made for a park shelter to replace the residence, using insurance funds made available after the building was declared a total loss. The Civic Garden Centre now has new headquarters in the building adjacent to the parking lot. Contemporary park structures were designed by Raymond Moriyama. Pause here a while for refreshments.

After leaving the Gardens at the Lawrence Avenue exit, turn left toward Bayview Avenue and take the first turn on the left, The Bridle Path. Follow this road to Park Lane Circle and then follow the total extent of the Circle to the intersection of the Post Road, returning easterly along the Post Road once more to the Bridle Path.

This area, despite stringent zoning restrictions, has virtually every known style of house architecture, ranging in price from $250,000 to more than $2 million. The disparate architectural expression of each house is saved from visual conflict because of the extensive acreage and landscaping surrounding the majority of homes. It is an interesting social commentary on building tastes of upper income Torontonians in the post-war period.

An extension of this tour could be made through the Wilket Creek Valley north of Lawrence Avenue and the Edwards Gardens to the estate of E.P. Taylor. All of this 55-acre estate (not including Winfields Farm, which has since been subdivided) was turned over to the North York park system by Taylor when he moved to the Bahamas in 1968. A 30-acre park along the Wilket Creek Valley is being developed right now as parkland; the rest will be when Taylor's immediate family no longer lives there, or in 50

Rear view of the Ontario Science Centre

offices, the headquarters of the Presbyterian Church, and a complex of data processing centres probably unequalled in Canada. At the east end of Wynford Drive is the Japanese Canadian Cultural Centre, again designed by Raymond Moriyama, and very worthy of a visit. Immediately to the south is the Holiday Inn, by the same architect, and here every attempt has been made to retain the trees and other natural amenities of the site.

Follow Wynford Drive along its full extent and return to Don Mills Road. Turn north to Greenbelt Drive, where a number of award-winning buildings may be found in close proximity to each other. The fact that outstanding and early post-war row housing by James Murray and Henry Fliess can exist within easy proximity to several Parkin-designed industrial buildings is a tribute to the planning constraints established from the outset by the Don Mills Development Corporation. Many of these buildings have, however, been somewhat compromised by thoughtless additions that do not maintain the character of the initial building concept, notably the Ortho Pharmaceutical building at Greenbelt and Don Mills Road.

To the north is the Don Mills Shopping Centre which, through its successive stages, no longer follows the original precision of its master plan. It is interesting, nonetheless, as one of the earliest malls in Canada.

Nearby are a series of small and large buildings, each in themselves of varying interest, probably more noted for the generous amount of space surrounding them than for any intrinsic architectural merit. A tour of the four quadrants of Don Mills is recommended. This can best be done by following the Donway. On this tiny road many of the important public facilities of Don Mills are located: an elementary school, a church, the major shopping centre, post office, public safety building and the inevitable curling rink.

The earliest quadrant was the north-west. From it one can sense the gradual appreciaion of public standards through the successive phases of building in the entire community through to Don Mills in its final phases in the Parkway West. This latter complex of high-rise and condominium row housing, all of very high standard, was undertaken by many of Toronto's best known housing specialists, Klein, Sears and Murray, Fliess.

While the defects of Don Mills may be readily apparent with the passage of almost 25 years since conceptual designs were presented, its outstanding characteristics can be perhaps best appreciated through the fact that much later peripheral development to the north — and to the east particularly — represent a vast decline in architectural and planning values. Many of these areas claim to be "Don Mills" in real estate columns, but one can promptly realize that they are the product of lesser standards and lesser imagination.

Top left: IOF Building
Top right: Flemingdon
Bottom left: Southills Village
Bottom right: Serena Gundy Park

Along the Escarpment

BY COLIN VAUGHAN
AND ANNABEL SLAIGHT

Many Toronto residential areas are a curious mixture of past and present but there is probably none more curious than the collection of neighborhoods along the Davenport Ridge. By exploring the bluffs of ancient Lake Ontario (just below St. Clair) you will find early farmhouses, a castle, a communal private estate, millionaires' mansions, finely rehabilitated middle-income housing and spruced up ticky-tacky. If you're interested in houses, new or old, and in how individual imagination and community spirit can keep neighborhoods thriving, a walk along the escarpment, with forays into its unique little residential developments, can be a delightful adventure.

Aside from being able to see interesting communities, the walk provides a lesson in how geographic features stimulate development. Of Toronto's three most important natural attractions — the lake, the escarpment, and the ravines — this area boasts two. And glimpses of the water are never far away. When Edwardian real estate brokers started to carve up the hillside estates of the previous century for their middle income clientele they must have had a heyday. They advertised a "magnificent view of the city and Lake Ontario, ideal wooded lots, drives, roads and avenues unsurpassed, and choice building restrictions." No wonder the ridge population grew by leaps and bounds.

Although the escarpment runs from the Yonge Street area to the western edge of the city, the most interesting stretch is from Gallows Hill at Yonge and Farnham (where allegedly in 1837 two men were hanged following a farcical attempt at battle by William Lyon Mackenzie's rebels) to Hillcrest Park just west of Christie with its unequalled panoramic view of the city.

Only the most adventuresome should tackle the suggested route in one trip — it takes about six hours at a leisurely pace. Better to plan a number of outings, and when you've had enough for one day, nip up to the St. Clair streetcar or, farther west, down to Dupont and the bus. Both will take you to the subway.

Being primarily a tour through a residential area there are few restaurants along the way. The number of eating places at Yonge and St. Clair is increasing all the time, however, and

Top left: Woodlawn Avenue gardens; Top right: House at 44 Farnham; Bottom left: De La Salle boy's school; Bottom right: Meisterschaft College.

MacPherson Avenue

there's always the varied fare of The Ports at Yonge and Walker. The best idea, weather permitting, may be to pack a lunch. Once you cross Avenue Road there are some excellent picnic spots.

On the way south to Farnham Avenue, and the start of this tour, poke into some of the stores along Yonge. This shopping area in the past few years has become quite sophisticated. Take a look also at St. Michael's Cemetery (access is between the hardware store and barber shop). It is an unusual back yard to high-rise office towers.

Farnham (two blocks south of St. Clair), like many streets in Deer Park South, was named for the earliest settler's estate, and most of these early estates were named for towns in England. While walking west along Farnham, down Woodlawn, and west on Walker you no doubt will find many "favorite" houses. What you see becomes even more fascinating when you realize that 20 years ago this area was extremely run down. A tremendous renaissance occurred throughout the 1960s. Deer Park South is still typical of the many neighborhoods, however, fighting for their existence.

A number of architects have homes in this area, although it is often difficult to distinguish them from the exciting examples of "folk" architecture. Architects' houses are at 31, 44, 50, 150 Farnham and 23, 59, 63, 85 Woodlawn.

One architect's house you should be

A home on Walker Avenue

sure to note is at 50 Farnham. It belongs to Geoff Armstrong. Farnham Lodge — as it used to be called — was originally a rough cast frame house and pre-dates subdivision of the street by 70 years. Its original occupant, Deer Park's first pharmacist, Edward Hooper located there in 1832.

The house, tucked in next door at 52, was once Farnham Lodge's coach house.

The other truly historic home in this neighborhood is at 35 Woodlawn. It was built by Chancellor William Hume Blake about 1830. Because it was the first house in the neighbor-

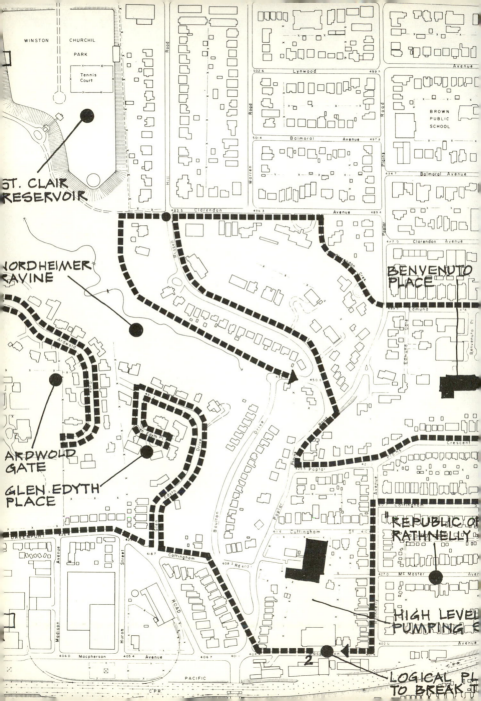

WINSTON CHURCHIL PARK

Tennis Court

ST. CLAIR RESERVOIR

NORDHEIMER RAVINE

BENVENUTO PLACE

ARDWOLD GATE

GLEN EDYTH PLACE

REPUBLIC OF RATHNELLY

HIGH LEVEL PUMPING E

LOGICAL PL TO BREAK T

2

BROWN PUBLIC SCHOOL

Lynwood

Balmoral   Avenue

Balmoral   Avenue

Clarendon   Avenue

Clarendon   Avenue

Avenue

Road

Road

Road

Plains   Road

Warren

Edmund

Benvenuto   Pl.

Ardwold

Crescent

Poplar

Cottingham

McMaster   Aver

Avenue

Cottingham

Boulton   Drive

Glen

Drive

Glen   Edyth   Drive

DAVENPORT

Madison   Avenue

Huron   Street

RCAD

Cottingham

Macpherson   Avenue

PACIFIC

CPR

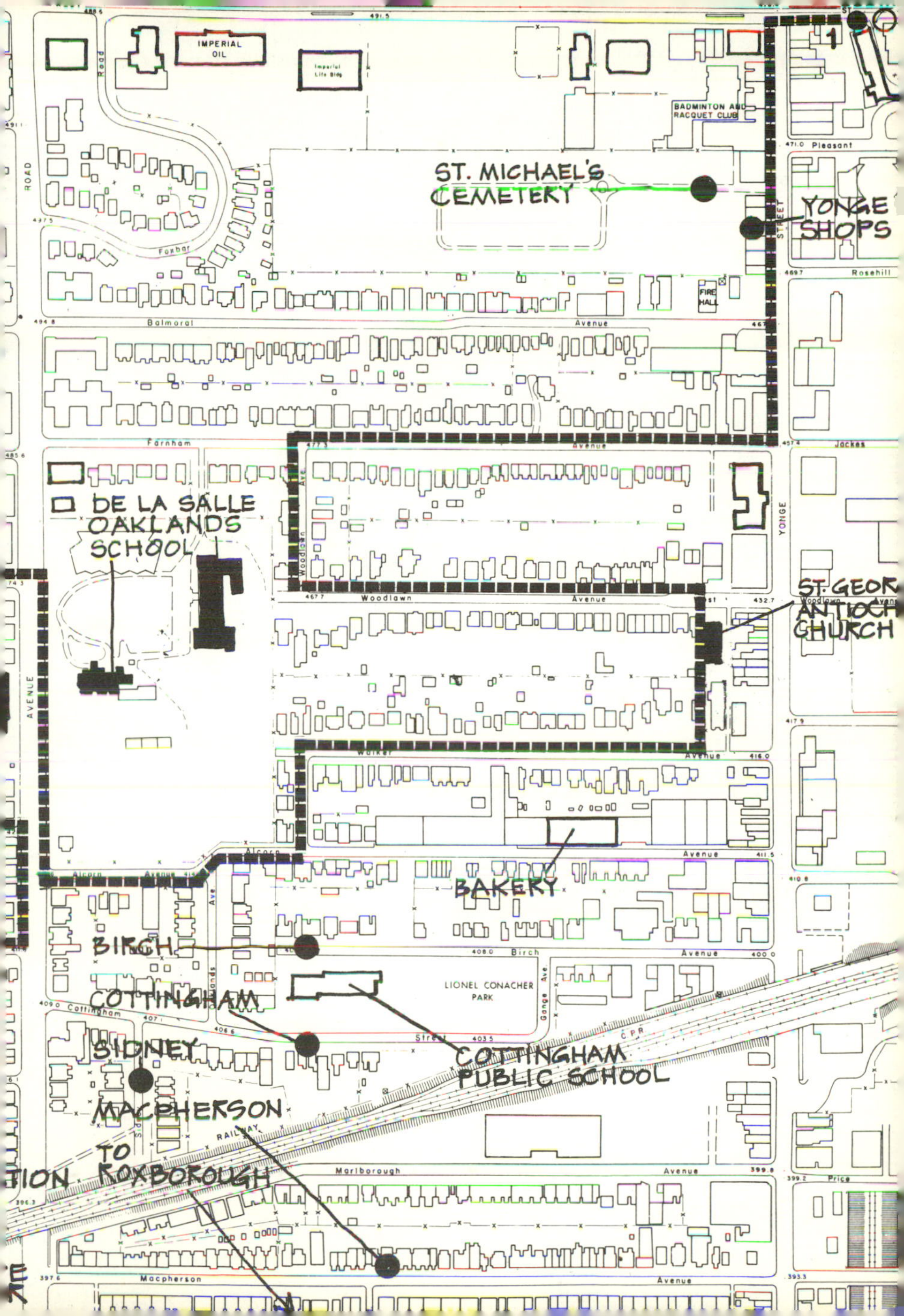

IMPERIAL
OIL

Imperial
Life Bldg

BADMINTON AND
RACQUET CLUB

Pleasant

ST. MICHAEL'S
CEMETERY

YONGE
SHOPS

Rosehill

FIRE
HALL

Balmoral   Avenue

Farnham

Jackes

DE LA SALLE
OAKLANDS
SCHOOL

Woodlawn   Avenue

ST. GEOR
ANTIOCH
CHURCH

AVENUE

Walker   Avenue

BAKERY

Alcorn   Avenue

Ave

Avenue

BIRCH

Birch   Avenue

COTTINGHAM

LIONEL CONACHER
PARK

Gange Ave

CPR

SIDNEY

Cottingham   Street

COTTINGHAM
PUBLIC SCHOOL

MACPHERSON

RAILWAY

TO
ROXBOROUGH

Marlborough   Avenue

Price

TION

Macpherson   Avenue

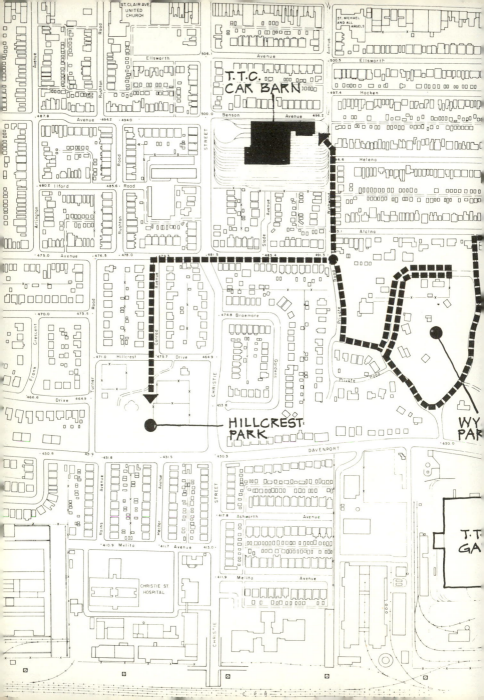

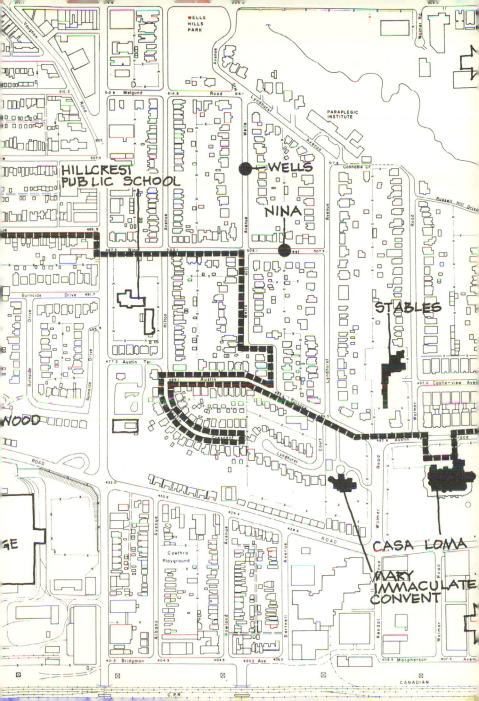

WELLS

NINA

HILLCREST
PUBLIC SCHOOL

STABLES

CASA LOMA

MARY
IMMACULATE
CONVENT

hood, and now sits not on the street but right in the centre of the block, present owners Mr. and Mrs. Guy Saunders have the properties of 24 neighbors completely surrounding them. If you cut through to Walker Avenue via the footpath between St. George Antiochian Church and number 13 Woodlawn, you can peek through the gardens to see how the neighborhood had to grow around the Saunders' house.

On Walker and Alcorn, which meets it, are more recently renovated houses. They also were built at the turn of the century but on narrower frontages than those on the choicer properties up the hill.

If you have time to spare, extend your walk down Oaklands Avenue to Cottingham, Sidney, Birch and Mac-Pherson and Roxborough below the railway tracks. All of these streets have their share of interesting old homes recently revitalized. Now head out to Avenue Road.

The large "gingerbread" building perched at the top of the Avenue Road Hill is De La Salle, a Catholic boys' private school. It was built in 1860 as "Oaklands" the home of businessman, politician and Methodist lay preacher Senator John Macdonald. The tracery work on this house is quite remarkable.

Across Avenue Road, off Edmund Avenue, is Benvenuto Place and one of the first Toronto apartment buildings designed in the post war "English" style. Architect Peter Dickinson was part of the small group that took Toronto architecture out of the 19th century. This high-rental apartment building will probably be considered an important work some day — it enhances rather than dominates its neighborhood.

Heading west along Edmund and across Poplar Plains Road, you now enter one of Toronto's poshest areas. Most houses are huge and grounds are meticulously kept. Cut through the secluded Clarendon Crescent and emerge on Clarendon Avenue. There are some attractive new townhouses here and the grand brick building on the south side is a school where the Bank of Commerce trains its managers.

At the end of Clarendon is the St. Clair Reservoir and the Nordheimer ravine. There used to be a river through here before it was diverted underground as part of the sewer system. This park also was one of the finest nature areas in the city until it was cleared for the construction of the Spadina transit line — the subway tunnel is under the grassed floor of the ravine. Today it is still a great place for a picnic and an even greater place to toboggan. Tomorrow, the Spadina Expressway could snake through. Although the road was once halted by citizen action, there has been pressure to revive it.

Next on this tour is the "Republic of Rathnelly," home to many artists, architects, academics and media people. To get there follow either route on the map: through the ravine to Poplar Plains Road or down Russell Hill Road. Watch street signs carefully to get to Poplar Plains Crescent.

This little pocket of streets, from Poplar Plains Crescent to MacPherson, is considered by residents not to be part of Canada. They seceded in 1967 as a Centennial project and Rathnelly citizens still carry "passports". While on the surface this is a joke, Rathnelly-ites say secession has brought many benefits: the neighborhood has been consolidated; there is great community spirit; and residents have been able to use the "republic" as a lever to get a playground established in the grounds of the High Level Pumping Station and a car park at the foot of Rathnelly Avenue. If you are very lucky you'll hit Rathnelly at annual festival time — it's held every 18 months.

Rathnelly is a logical place to break this tour. If you choose to stop now you can catch a bus on Avenue Road. If you decide to carry on, follow the route on the map over to Glen Edyth Drive and back up to the top of the escarpment. This cul-de-sac, and the one west of it at Ardwold Gate, are probably seen more by visitors to the city than Torontonians. Both contain fairly new houses, and somehow, in spite of the lack of tropical vegetation, are reminiscent of Bel Air and Beverly Hills in Los Angeles.

On your way to Ardwold Gate you pass Casa Loma and this 98-room "dream" of Sir Henry Pellatt is certainly worth a visit. So are the stables reached via an 800-foot tunnel.

Sir Henry, financier, royalist and devoted military officer, built his castle as if to withstand a siege. Foundations are 45 feet deep; between each floor there is a four-foot crawl space to permit easy access to electrical wiring and plumbing, and the main floor, of reinforced concrete covered with teak, is strong enough to support heavy military equipment. Construction of Casa Loma was begun in 1911 but halted during World War I. Since 1937 it has been operated by the Kiwanis Club of West Toronto as a tourist attraction.

The house next to the castle with the magnificent porte-cochère, at 285 Spadina, was built in 1866 but has been altered and added-to many times since then. You can peek at the gardens of this lovely estate from the end of Ardwold Gate.

Casa Loma's neighbor to the west is the Sisters Servants of Mary Immaculate Convent at 5 Austin Terrace. Architect for the castle, E.J. Lennox, built this house for himself from materials left over from construction of the castle. Children from all parts of the city now come here for singing and piano lessons.

Continuing west, you come to the more modest but still charming streets of Wells Hill, Hilton Avenue, Austin Crescent and Nina which takes you out to Bathurst.

Alcina Avenue, on the other side of Bathurst, will take you to the private communal estate of Wychwood Park. You can enter the park through a small gate and a footpath between 77 and 83 Alcina. Note, by the way, number 41 Alcina as you pass by: this is the home of well-known artist York Wilson.

Wychwood Park, named for Wychwood Forest in Oxfordshire, was founded in 1891 as a self-operated, self-contained artists' colony by a group headed by artist Marmaduke Matthews. It is still — although on a much larger scale — an autonomous community. Owners pay general taxes to the city, but, through a board of trustees, maintain their own roads and purchase their own utilities.

Residents encourage visitors on foot but will shut the entrance gates if they seem to be invaded by aimless vehicular traffic.

Most houses in the park are charming but the only really significant one is Marmaduke Matthew's farmhouse built in 1874. It has been meticulously restored by its present owner.

Perhaps more fascinating than the individual houses is the atmosphere of the park itself. Before leaving be sure to take the loop down to Taddle Creek and the Pond, well stocked with goldfish (put there by a young man off to World War I the story goes). In winter, residents hop the fence to skate here — among them you may see Marhsall McLuhan who lives in the park at number 3.

There are two kinds of finales to this walk. One is for streetcar buffs: the TTC car barns are just up Wychwood Avenue. Otherwise, continue along Tyrrel across Christie and down Conrad into Hillcrest Park, for an unequalled view of the city.

Casa Loma

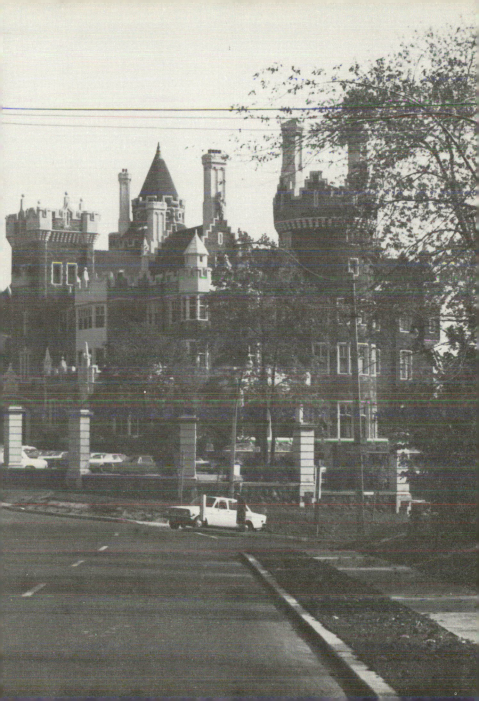

City Excursions

UNION STATION

Union Station at Front and Bay is described by the president of the Toronto Branch of the Ontario Architectural Conservancy, Doug Richardson, as "one of the most splendid examples of its type and architecture on the face of the earth." Whether you agree or not, for 48 years as the transportation hub of the country, it has played an important part in Canadian history. See it now and rejoice, for its fate has been decided. It was in danger of being demolished to make way for the office towers of the huge CN-CP Metro Centre development — but citizen action has saved it. When you stand in the 250-foot main concourse, (the Great Hall as some grandiloquently refer to it) be sure to look overhead at the 88-foot high arched ceiling. It is easy to see why some call this palatial building a "cathedral of travel and traffic."

SCARBOROUGH COLLEGE

Scarborough College, at 1265 Military Trail in Scarborough, is a building that put Canadian architecture on the world map. Designed in 1965 by Page and Steele in Association with John Andrews Architects, it was developed with the idea that the "modern academic program as established for Scarborough, geared to contemporary teaching methods and techniques such as television, could not best be served by established design concepts based on traditional teaching philosophy." So the result was a bunker-like string of buildings huddled on the edge of a ravine and joined together by a climate-controlled pedestrian walkway.

ONTARIO PLACE, CNE, MARINE MUSEUM

Eb Zeidler, the architect for the 90-acre Ontario Place on Toronto's waterfront, across from the Canadian National Exhibition grounds, lumps this Ontario showcase together with the London Crystal Palace, the Eiffel Tower and the Buckminster Fuller dome at Expo '67 as examples of "how buildings symbolize the aspirations of their time." As well as giving a glimpse of tomorrow, Ontario Place gives at very little cost to visitors — terrific entertainment. There are boats to watch or ride in, movies and concerts to see, exhibits, places for kids to play

Top: Black Creek Pioneer Village
Bottom: Ontario Place

High Park

and you can even just sit in the sun and sip beer.

Ontario Place, as well as being of interest in its own right, is significant for its role as catalyst for redevelopment of the old Ex, on Lakeshore Boulevard at the foot of Strachan Avenue. A number of architects are already preparing drawings and the facelift is soon to come.

In addition to tomorrow and today, there are some fascinating glimpses of yesterday in this area. The 350-acre CNE site, has historical connections predating the earliest shows. It was the battlefield on which 62 Canadians were killed and 34 wounded when Americans invaded the city on April 27, 1813 and occupied it for 11 days. Earlier, the land had been a French fort, burned in 1759 to keep it from falling into British hands. Today a stone cairn marks this spot, and on the grounds is the Maritime Museum, featuring displays of these periods.

YORK UNIVERSITY, BLACK CREEK VILLAGE

York University grew out of the reasoned need for a second Toronto university and was incorporated in 1959, though classes did not begin on the Glendon campus until 1961. The first buildings on the main Downsview campus, 4700 Keele Street, were completed four years later. Now this part of the university — including Atkinson and Winters Colleges and the curious Burton Auditorium — has grown to approximately 25 structures. All are decidedly urban in design as it was thought that the university will one day soon be surrounded by the on-pushing city and should blend in with those future surroundings.

Not far away, at Steeles and Jane, and 30 minutes by car from City Hall, is a project whose style and purpose in design is the opposite. Intended to show us the Metro area as it once was— not as it will be — Black Creek Pioneer Village began in 1954 when a forerunner of the Metropolitan Toronto and Region Conservation Authority acquired 14 acres on which sat a Pennsylvania German log barn built in 1809. Around this a town has been created, with approximately 25 other buildings from the 1793-1867 period being transported from other parts of the province and restored.

HIGH PARK, COLBORNE LODGE

In 1955, the City decided that Toronto's largest park, High Park, should be made attractive to all citizens rather than the select few who found it of interest in an undeveloped state. Since then, one of the most outstanding floral displays on this continent has been developed here and activities for people have been provided, from summer month concerts to toboggan hills and nature trails.

Contrary to what some people think, the 339-acre park was not entirely donated by the John G. Howard estate.

Howard did, however, donate the central portion of the park but did so with the stipulation that "consumption of malt or spirited liquors" be prohibited. You can still visit the picturesque 1836 Howard house, Colborne Lodge (on Howard Road in High Park) now operated as a histori-

cal museum. Howard, by the way, was an architect of some repute as well as being a city surveyor and an engineer. He was drawing master at Upper Canada College for 23 years.

ART GALLERY OF ONTARIO

A logical excursion to a trip through Chinatown is a walk further west on Dundas to the Art Gallery of Ontario at Grange Park. It's one of the biggest and best art galleries in North America and houses, among other things, the largest public collection of Henry Moore's works in the Western hemisphere.

While at the AGO be sure to visit The Grange, the oldest brick house remaining in central Toronto. For years it housed the Gallery offices and a tearoom but now has been restored by the Women's Committee to a living museum.

The Grange was built in 1817 by D'Arcy Boulton, Jr., when Toronto was still the Town of York. Under the Boulton family it became the centre of social and political life in Upper Canada. Boulton's widow, who inherited the house, married Goldwin Smith in 1875 and the traditions of The Grange were broadened by the intellectual pursuits of Smith, the distinguished Oxford scholar. It was decided shortly before Mrs. Goldwin Smith died to will the house to the new Art Museum of Toronto and, in 1911, The Grange became the permanent residence of the art gallery.

Architectural credits

Alexandra Park, *Jerome Markson Architects, Klein and Sears, Webb Zerafa Menkes*
Ansheiminsk Synagogue, St. Andrews Street, *Kaplan and Sprachman*
Bishop's Palace, adjacent to St. Michael's Cathedral, *William Thomas*
Bank of Montreal, Yonge and Front, *Frank Darling and S.G. Curry*
Bata International Headquarters, *John B. Parkin Associates*
Benvenuto Place, *Peter Dickenson*
Berkeley Street, Offices and Showrooms, 55-79, *Joan Burt*
Canadian Imperial Bank of Commerce, Market Branch, *John Chapman*
Canadian Imperial Bank of Commerce, Yonge and Wellington, *Henry Langley*
Casa Loma, *E.J. Lennox*
City Hall, new, *Viljo Revell, John B. Parkin Associates.*
City Hall, Toronto's First, *Henry Bower Lane*
Central Technical Institute, Art Studios, *Fairfield and DuBois*
Colonnade, *Gerald Robinson*
Commerce Court, *Darling and Pearson, 1930, Page and Steele, 1972, Consultant, I.M. Pei,* New York
David Mirvish Gallery, *John Andrews, Architects*
Donald Summerville Olympic Pool, *Wilson and Newton*
Don Mills Shopping Centre, *John B. Parkin and Associates and Fisher Tedman and Glaister*
Edwards Gardens, Park Structures,

Raymond Moriyama
Flemingdon Park, *Irving Grossman*
Four Seasons-Sheraton Hotel, *Searle Wilbee Rowland*
Gooderham and Worts Distillery, *David Roberts*
Gooderham Building, *William Kaufman*
Greenwood Race Track, *Earle C. Morgan and Page and Steele*
Hart House, *Sproatt and Rolph*
Holiday Inn, Don Valley Parkway, *Raymond Moriyama*
Holy Trinity Church, *Henry Bower Lane*
IBM Canada Headquarters, *John B. Parkin Associates*
Imperial Oil Regional Headquarters, *John B. Parkin Associates*
Inn on the Park, *Webb Zerafa Menkes Housden*
Japanese Canadian Cultural Centre, *Raymond Moriyama*
Karelia International, *Janis Kravis*
King's College, *Thomas Young*
Knox College, 1875, *Smith and Gemmell*
Knox College, 1915, *Darling and Pearson*
Little Trinity Church, *Henry Bower Lane*
Metro Court House, new, *Marani Rounthwaite and Dick*
Metropolitan United Church, *Henry Langley, J. Gibb Morton*
Nursewood Road, number 2, *Tampold and Wells*
Necropolis, *Henry Langley*